George provides a raw and ɛ
with mental illness. She shares
highlighting some of her sympto.
and early adulthood. Helen Joy describes her attempts to get treatment
and the obsta-cles she encountered each time.

Yellow Tulips provides an accurate reflection of the symp-toms of
Bipolar Affective Disorder I, diagnostic challeng-es, and treatment
concerns. This is required reading in my psychiatric mental health
nurse practitioner course to pro-vide students an opportunity to enhance
their knowledge as well as understanding the patient experience in the
mental health system. This is an excellent and authentic resource!

— Evelyn Parrish, PhD, PMHNP-BC, FAANP

Associate Professor • Director of Accreditation and Strategic

Outcomes, University of Kentucky College of Nursing

I was torn between rushing through every page and need-ing to put it
down to catch my breath and feel the depths of pain and joy on every
page. As a therapist, I am famil-iar with deep suffering: It is the world
in which I live each day. Helen Joy has a way of pulling back the veil,
inviting all of us to see and feel more deeply what it's like to live with
bipolar disorder, to stay alive, and to fight for healing and hope. I
have known Helen Joy a long time and am a better person for it. I am
grateful that Yellow Tulips allows more people to learn what Helen
Joy lives—the grace that matches the pain.

— Elizabeth Gillespie, LMFT

YELLOW TULIPS

one woman's quest for hope and healing
in the darkness of bipolar disorder

Helen Joy George

Mountain Page Press

Hendersonville, NC

Published 2019 by The Cheerful Word
Reprinted 2021 by Mountain Page Press

ISBN 978-1-952714-08-5
Copyright © 2019, 2021 **Helen Joy George**

Cover photo by Rachael MacPhee
Cover design by Meghan McDonald
Interior book design by Daniel Ojedokun

For information, contact the publisher at:
Mountain Page Press
118 5th Ave. W.
Hendersonville, NC 28792

Visit: www.mountainpagepress.com

This is a work of creative non-fiction. All of the events in this memoir are true to the best of the author's memory. Some names and identifying features have been changed to protect the identity of certain parties.
The views expressed in this memoir are solely those of the author.

Dedicated to the little girl who never gives up.

I am in awe of you.

DISCRETION ADVISED

This book contains stories relating to suicide, violence, sexual abuse, alcoholism, drug abuse, and cutting.

While the author has taken great lengths to ensure the subject matter is dealt with in a compassionate and respectful manner, it may be troubling for some readers.

CONTENTS

PART ONE

PART TWO

PREFACE

There is nothing to writing. All you do is sit down at a typewriter and bleed. – Ernest Hemingway

This book lived inside of me. I sat down, and bit by bit it poured onto my paper, sometimes so furiously that I don't recall writing it at all. Now that it is all out, I feel like I can breathe again.

For as long as I can remember, I've always wanted to write a memoir. As a little girl, I used to lie in the grass and look up into the blue sky and dream of one day writing about my crazy life, because even back then I knew there was something special about it. I was going to name the book The *Gypsy Mobile,* referencing the gypsy lifestyle my family lived. I gathered stories as a young child and kept them close to my heart like cherished possessions. These memories are heartbreaking, hilarious, and magical. Some are utterly un-believable. It wasn't until I was thirty-one that I felt that my stories were ready to be born, when I was just emerging from a year of fighting for my life in the mental health care system.

Throughout this book, I tell stories of my childhood, my first love, my teenage marriage, my rough start into motherhood, and my descent into the darkness of mental illness. Several names have been changed and a few threads pulled from the tapestry of my life to protect the identities of the brave and the stories that are not mine to tell.

The stories in this book are frozen in time. Many situa-tions no longer exist, many relationships have changed. But this is how it was when it happened.

I wrote this book to heal my broken heart. I wrote it to laugh. I wrote it to help others understand what it's like to live with mental illness. But mostly, I wrote it because I was longing for beauty and hope to arise. And once I wrote it all down, they did.

PART

1

DAD

He smelled like concrete and Old Spice. His tattered work clothes were always covered in a thin layer of grime, but I thought he was the most handsome man I'd ever seen. Rugged. Hardy. His red curly hair was always playfully tousled, coming down over his eye, as if he were perpetually winking. His nose was covered in freckles, which is something he passed down to me—my inheritance of sorts. He gave me something else besides the freckles. Whenever you looked into his pale, blue eyes, you could sense longing and sadness. I feel it in every photograph I've seen of him. I have it too.

One of the most legendary stories I've heard about my father was when, at age fifteen, he got so angry with his parents that he tried to paddle his surfboard from the shoreline of Sullivan's Island, South Carolina, near his home, miles out to a cargo ship heading to Africa. He made it onto the ship, and while he didn't make it to Africa, he landed in the pages of the Charleston Post and Courier the following day: "Young Surfer Rescued." When my grandfather passed away fifty years later,

I received a box of newspaper clippings. I discovered that my dad's ocean-deep resolve enabled him to accomplish some impressive things. The following year, Dad decided to shirk all of his high school sports, grow out his hair, and become the best surfer in the Southeast. He made and kept a vow to surf every day for 365 days and ended up winning the state championship five times in a row.

I used to watch him surf, and I would feel so happy. His eyes gazed at the horizon, his body relaxed as he was gently soothed by the rocking waves he let pass. It was the only place I ever saw peace in him.

In the South, and in the church, we were taught that men held all the authority in a household. When I was tiny, Mama taught me about the authority hierarchy: "God is in charge of Daddy, Daddy is in charge of Mommy, Mommy is in charge of you," she said, as we pasted together a mobile to illustrate the idea.

"But I want to boss someone!" I protested in my tiny voice.

Mama glanced over and saw some animal stickers from our craft basket and offered, "The birds. You can boss the birds."

My dad was different from other church men. He was gentle— defeated, maybe—but gentle.

I'll never forget being about ten years old and having to get a spanking. Dad didn't do much of the spanking in our house, so this was a rare occasion. He walked me into our pink sitting room so he could administer my punishment, shut the door, and whispered to me with eyes twinkling, "Just yell." Then he wrapped his strong arms around me and hit a book on the table. I yelled out, trying to contain my giggles. We did that a few more times till we knew that we would satisfy Mom. He gave me a hug and I walked out, trying to mask the lack of repentance on my face.

My mom wanted to be submissive as she had been taught, although Dad never required that of her. Others saw his gentleness as laziness. People around him viewed his God-given tenderness as weak and ungodly. I loved him just the way he was.

Dad was a straight-up genius. While not the best student, he was sharp with anything that kindled his interest. He was also deeply creative. His creativity took root with building and designing stunning, round domes across the US. His mind never quit; he was always thinking of a different way to do things, a better way to do things. He was a science whiz and obsessed with empirical facts that proved God's existence. He truly was a brilliant creation.

Dad was father to five girls: Helen Joy, Katie Beth, Julianna, Georgia Ann, and Sarah Grace. Even though he was an incredible human, Dad did not parent much. A lot of my memories of him at home are of him sleeping or of vacant eyes staring back at me when I tried to talk to him. He was worn down by labor and weary in his bones from trying to be someone he wasn't. He had secrets that weighed him down, and working himself to death was easier than being present. He was riddled with depression and bouts of mania that left his eyes bloodshot—mental illness back before it had a name.

My real dad surfaced once in a while with a short burst of energy, a frantic grab for connection. Sometimes he would tickle us while putting on our Sunday shoes till we were crying with laughter. Sometimes he would throw us out into the ocean and bring us back to shore, only to throw us back out again. Dad had an armful of jokes that he kept handy and would pull them out with a dimpled wink. Every so often, he would gather his energy and pick up his shiny harmonica. He would start off with a chug chug, like a small train, and soon all his little tow-headed girls would come twirling in their twirliest dresses as he played "Orange Blossom Special" through his wide smile. His eyes would twinkle.

I ache thinking about him. I wish he were here, wrestling my boys to the ground and laughing as he tickles them. I ache for him to play his harmonica as my daughter spins around in her twirly dress. I ache for that twinkle.

Dad died when I was thirteen. Well, he's not exactly dead, but he might as well be.

His brain has been carved out, with a deep groove where memories should be. This groove was created by a nail going from one side of his head to the other, right at his temples, shot by his own hand from a nail gun.

Today my father sits in a home for the forgotten, twiddling his thumbs in a dark room lit by a TV. He's a shell—the body of my dad and the mind of a child. He is always scheming to get his old life back: a wife, his career, his surfing. While he waits for a future that will never arrive, he works as a bag boy at a local grocery store. I've seen him in action there, watching as he stumbles around doing simple tasks.

The Christmas just weeks before he shot himself, I spent every free moment I had on his lap, my awkward thirteen-year-old body draped over him the way a tiny child would do. We didn't talk, but in the silence somehow I knew that something wasn't right and he needed me. He was dirty and slumped over—full of defeat.

On New Year's Eve, as 1999 approached, my mom and sisters and I gathered under a great big clock in downtown Charleston to await midnight with thousands of other festive people. Dad was at a job two hours away. While I waved bright neon glow sticks through the night air, my mother was on the phone with my dad, trying to convince him to stay alive. None of us kids had a clue this was happening—she was so good at protecting us. Without warning, she abruptly dragged us away from the ball drop, saying she wanted us to pray at home together at midnight. Mom stayed on the phone with Dad during the entire thirty-minute drive home. She succeeded, at least temporarily; he didn't kill himself that night. Early the next morning, she drove the two hours to be with him. Despite her best efforts, a week later he would follow through.

My mom spent the entire week before it happened at Dad's job site, cooking, tying steel, holding him throughout the night. She played worship music to dispel the hallucinations that robbed him of sleep. Early on the morning of January 8, she awoke to an empty bed, and she knew.

She found him in his work trailer with a suicide message slurred into a tape recorder and five small hearts welded out of steel. One for each of his girls and nothing for Mom.

I was downstairs in the home we shared with our grandparents, a state away. We were excitedly packing to go see Mom and Dad at the job site, because a week had gone by since Mom had left. I was in charge of the four younger girls, including baby Sarah Grace, and I was scurrying around, gathering things to bring with us. All of a sudden, I heard my grandmother Helen let out the most inhuman sound—and a scream, "Oh my God! No!" I heard her small body crumple onto the floor above me. I heard her call out, "Your father has been shot. I don't know if he's alive."

I fell to the cold floor at the foot of the stairs and cried out to God like a wounded animal. For a while, time stood still and I felt like I was floating, then panic ensued. Within the hour our home was filled with adults pouring in from all over town. They spoke in muted whispers as the kids, left alone downstairs, tried to sort out the details of what had happened. In the end, we decided that some man must have shot our dad. My sisters, cousin, and I plotted how to find that man and make him pay.

Dad was alive in the intensive care unit after bleeding for hours and being brought back to life twice. We didn't get to see him for two days. Someone had given me the soundtrack to Prince of Egypt as an "I'm so sorry your dad got shot" gift. There's a song on it called "Miracles." I helped my sisters into our grandparents' car and listened to that song on repeat on my Walkman the whole two-hour drive. I was looking out the window at the blurring landscape, praying and believing that my dad would live. I believed in a miracle.

When we arrived at the hospital I breathed in that smell— overcooked food mixed with antiseptic and bodily fluids. All of these memories are tinged with that smell. We finally saw our mama and gathered around her on the floor like five flower petals. She told us that our dad shot himself with a nail gun on purpose. She didn't know if he would survive or just be a vegetable. Grasping for signs that God could hear our prayers, Mom read a verse out of the Bible that said, "he protects all his bones, not one of them will be broken."

Dad had shot five times through his hand to numb himself for this attempt at his life. None of the bones in his hand were broken, so my sisters and I drew an "X" on the places on our hands where the nails had entered his. It was our sign to remember miracles, and we did it every day for nearly a year.

When they finally took us back to see him, I noticed his hair lay greasy and long on one side of the pillow, with his head shaved and displaying a fresh wound of staples on the other. A haze of sensations surrounded me: a thick blue tube down his throat, that smell, those beeps of the machines keeping him alive. I stood there so small, so helpless as I watched his chest rise and fall to the sound of the sucking tube.

I wish we could have all leaned over and kissed him, whispered how much we loved and forgave him, and released him from this life, from this toil and weariness. Was it our prayers that tied him there?

For nearly a year my mother stayed by his side, rubbing in oils, giving supplements, practicing physical therapy. Months spent away from my sisters and me. Months hanging onto the hope of a wiggled toe, a hand squeeze, a sign that God was hearing our prayers. Sometimes on the weekends, someone would drive us girls up for a visit. We had the luxury of staying at the Ronald McDonald House, which is usually reserved for sick kids, but they made an exception for us. It was magical. There were cheerful murals in every room, more games and toys than we had ever seen, and the most delicious food delivered by local churches or families every night. We loved being there, but visiting Dad left a queasy feeling in my stomach that I could never shake. The person in that hospital bed wasn't him.

Once he finally left the hospital, he sat thin and empty in a wheelchair. We waited for his spirit to return, holding our breath as the new realities of living with someone with a traumatic brain injury set in.

I remember distinctly the day my father became my child. I had held out hope for so long that this wasted shell of a man would come to life again. We walked slowly on the beach as he dragged his leg behind him in the foam of the incoming tide. I reached out to grab his hand and peered at him curiously as he walked by my side. A huge ache overtook me as I realized my dad was gone. In that moment, I felt the father I loved, the man who used to toss me into the sea with his strong arms, slip gently away into it, never to return.

The year after Dad's injury, we started giving emotional testimonies at churches and around campfires about God's goodness and the miracle of my dad's life—how he had survived and how the bones in his hand had not been broken, just as promised in that Bible verse. Christians everywhere were praising God because of this miracle, and my faith felt alive and vigorous. In my young heart, I just knew that all of this hurt had happened for a reason.

Soon after we gave all of these testimonies, dark, painful secrets came out about my dad, from his own mouth. Things he had hidden away. He couldn't remember all of our names clearly, yet vivid memories of the past that came bubbling up to the surface. It didn't feel like a miracle then: my baby sister never knew him, we lost our mama for a year, and a great crack in my understanding of God had formed.

Today, the only traces I see of my dad are in the ink scrawlings up and down his arms calculating the distance to the galaxies, the long recitations of relativity that he has painstakingly memorized over the years, and his jokes—though forever repetitive.

It must be hell in his mind. Some days he sighs and says, "I wasn't planning to make it through that." Some days I sigh and think, "I wish he hadn't made it through that."

So many times I want to go back to that scared thirteen-year-old on the floor, crying out to God, and tell her to shut her mouth.

But if there is any redemption in his story, in his life, it's that it would one day save mine.

MAMA

I was born to a mama with a heart the size of our universe and an emptiness just as vast. I was her first baby and she endured a week of labor before I was placed in her trembling arms. Try as I might, my eight-pound-three-ounce self could never fill her void.

When my mother talks about her childhood, a gray veil drapes across her eyes. Even though there was good, it existed alongside great sorrow and the devastating loss of her innocence, which someone ripped from her chubby, little-girl fingers in the darkness—in the hidden parts—over and over again. It was this tragedy in her formative years that trapped her brain in childlike sensitivity. It also led her, at twelve years old, to stop eating—grasping for any control she could take back.

Mama grew up in Mississippi, the youngest of four children. Her father worked as a pastor, and her artistic mother led the life of a pastor's wife. They were both busy in the ministry, and my grandmother was also occupied with many hobbies. Surrounded by siblings and competing with God's work, Mama didn't feel very important. Still, Mama talks about the good times. About spending summers at a camp her father directed—where he was present and fun. About camping trips to the mountains with her family, their station wagon filled with blankets in the back for a bed.

Then there was Granny, my great-grandmother, who took a special shining to my mother. With Granny, Mama had a place. They did everything together: cooking, working in the garden, hauling water from the well, and bringing coal to their elderly neighbors.

When Mama met Dad, she was a mature-looking twelve-year-old and he was the new twenty-three-year-old youth pastor at her father's church. Mama was so tall that she towered awkwardly over everyone else her age. In school pictures she looks like a grown woman. In fact, when she walked into a brand-new school in the fifth grade, everyone mistook her for the new teacher. Despite her premature physical development, Mama was innocent and childlike.

On the day my parents met, Mama was playing the piano while Daddy asked her questions, intending to invite her on a date. After several minutes, he exclaimed, "Why, you're talking about the fifth grade like you are in it!"

"I am!" she retorted.

Shortly after they met, Dad left town to attend grad school in South Carolina. Despite her only knowing him for a short time, he had made a lasting impression on my mama. While he was away, Mama would save up her hard-earned babysitting money to make and mail him cookies, all in the name of friendship. In return, he'd send her hand-drawn cartoons and funny Valentine cards. When she turned eighteen, my father sent a letter asking her to fly across the country to visit him. Mom accepted his invitation and flew to Colorado Springs where he had recently moved to; this was the official beginning of their romance.

During their fervent courtship, they wrote each other endless love letters, stacks of which sit in the bottom of my hope chest. I have yellowing photos of them together—tanned, bright, exploring the mountain wilderness of Colorado in matching T-shirts and cowboy hats. In my favorite one, Mama, with her long, brown hair falling down her back, stares with her doe-like blue eyes at my dad taking her picture.

They ended up marrying when my mother was twenty years old and my dad was thirty-one. On their wedding night, after all of the festivities were over, Mom requested that they watch *Little House on the Prairie* and eat popcorn before falling asleep—a wall to protect her from her painful past.

As a child, I loved seeing my parents together. I would peek through the banister at the top of our stairs, craning my head for a view of them kissing. It seemed like a storybook romance, the actual living out of the happily-ever-after stories they read to me. I loved the way Mama's cheeks flushed as Dad scooped her up in his strong arms and the giggle that would spring out of her mouth. My sisters and I would craft homemade dates for them, playing restaurant complete with hand-drawn menus and lumpy soups.

Their story ended up the opposite of happily ever after—a story broken on the rocks, with secrets and lies exposed. It ended with a trail of history flying loose in the wind. But when I was growing up, it really was magical to me. I will clasp this truth tightly in my hands, just as I do a firefly in the summer, so no one can ever take it from me.

Mama raised and educated us while traveling around the country, following my dad as he built monolithic domes around the country. This lifestyle could have broken many women, but my mama soared. She filled the loneliness of being on the road with wonder and excitement. In every town we lived in, we'd scour the museums, national parks, and libraries, eagerly devouring everything we could learn. We'd always visit the gift shops, but instead of buying trinkets or toys, we'd all pick out a biography to read aloud together. That and a math book were our curriculum.

Even when I was young, during our travels it was clear to me that I had two moms: one was the adventurous rule breaker with a gleam in her eye, and the other was the proper mother and wife who lived to please others. One lived on the road, and the other lived in the refined and deeply religious town of Charleston, South Carolina. I would learn that I greatly preferred one over the other.

Mom read to us every night. We would all pile on her like a litter of puppies, and she would read for hours. This nighttime routine was one of the only constants of my childhood, and I treasure my memories of these times. I loved the way her voice sounded and how the vibrations of her words felt when I laid my head on her lap; I loved her gentle caress of my hair. My mind expanded and was saturated with the pictures and stories on each new page, and I felt safe. She created that nest every night; even when she was exhausted, even when she was broken. You see, Mama has a fire burning brightly inside of her: a fire for survival and for adventure. This flame has helped her navigate a life jammed full of heartache.

BEAUTIFUL CREATION

Have you ever watched a little girl in a dress twirl around the room? Eyes to the sky, hands thrown out wildly, beaming like the sun—she's captivating. It makes me ache. Sometimes a tear slips out and trickles into my smile as I watch my daughter twirl. She heals me, she kisses the scars. Every day I tell her, "You are a beautiful creation."

When I was a little girl, I was tiny and packed full of vibrancy. People were drawn to me, just as they are to my own girl. Mama said that walking through the store was difficult because strangers would stop to ooh and ahh over me. I parted the sea of people as I sashayed down the aisle. I engaged adults in conversation before I could walk. There are old VHS tapes of me performing and spinning with sophisticated abandon. There are accounts of my bold directing of plays. There was also that one time when I was eight and believed I could invent something to make me breathe underwater. I planted baby trees in a Coke bottle and taped a tube to my mouth and connected it to the bottle. Trees created oxygen, so I assumed they could keep me breathing while I discovered treasures under the lake for hours. I meticulously planned and worked on my creation for a week. I still have a picture that I adore of me standing proudly with my modified coke bottle. Freckles, streaked blond hair, and my dad's twinkly eyes. When I look at that photo, I am overwhelmed with love for that little girl.

I taught myself gymnastics by watching and rewatching tapes of the 1996 Olympic team performing in Atlanta, Georgia. I trained on our trampoline, on the grass, on a pull-up bar at a neighbor's house, and on a two-by-four balance beam Dad built for me, covered in scratchy gray carpet. After a few weeks of practicing and mastering a back handspring on my carpeted balance beam, I decided to sell my autograph to the neighbors: *Helen Joy Paul, future Olympian.* Bold. Fiery. I love her.

Ideas poured out of me. I would take my mom's film camera and set up a dramatic scene and pose for it, making my sisters snap the shutter. A photographer from the beginning, I was especially keen on creating scenes where I'd lie tragically dead in a sea of flowers à la *Anne of Green Gables.* I love her.

I was born with confidence inside. A beautiful confidence that was smashed when I stopped and heard the whispers "Too much, too much." Mostly people delighted in me, but whenever I let myself get lost in the glory of being who I was, I saw the looks and heard the whispers: "Too much. Too much. She's just too much." It started seeping into my bones.

I have piles of journals in my closet. Mismatched. Youthful. Plastic locks and Lisa Frank dolphins all the way up to college-ruled and leather-bound pieces. As I open each one, the words of self-loathing hit me like a brick wall. I'm heartbroken. How can a child hate who she is at such a young age? A hundred pages begging God to change me, to fix me. I must have been made wrong.

Why can't I be a gentle and quiet spirit like the Bible says??????
Why???

The summer I was sixteen, I was finally able to achieve an eating disorder. I had tried many times before and hadn't been able to make it past lunchtime. I eventually got down to one apple a day. The way my flesh disappeared each day made me feel gentle and quiet. The loss of energy made it impossible for me to shine my bright light. I had never felt more feminine, more godly. I had finally reduced myself to being palatable to others. My eating disorder didn't last but a month; emptiness didn't agree with me.

I have long lived with the notion that emptying myself is the only way to please certain people, the people I cared for the most. I've sought this hollowness through food restriction, biting my tongue so I couldn't speak, and concealing the savage hurt pulsing through me. Hiding, emptying, making myself small—these are things that I battle to this day. And truly, as soon as I empty myself, I fill right back up— an ever-bubbling spring of life. I don't stay empty for long.

I grew up being taught that women should be kept in a nice, neat box. But I did not fit. I could never quite bring myself to twist and contort, to reduce my exuberant self enough to squeeze into that box. And because I didn't fit, I never once had someone cup my face in their hands and say, "You are a beautiful creation," the way I tell my Lucy.

My own mother, a beautifully vibrant woman, seemed to be crushed by what we were taught in the church: that women should be gentle, quiet, meek, and not "too much." Once in a while, I'd see my mom's true self break out—in a spontaneous night swim, in a fit of laughter and giggling that ended in tears, in a thrilling quest she'd pursue. In those fleeting moments, she was beautiful and breathless. It was incredible to watch her in her own skin, in her own breath, in her own soul. Things were right in the world, if but for a brief moment. I remember feeling deep sorrow when I would watch her quietly slip back into the box of submission.

Thankfully, I was blessed with three special women who refused to be contained: my two grandmothers—I acquired a name from each one—and my great-aunt Lucy.

There was my grandmother Helen, my Dad's mom, barefoot and covered in wrinkles. She coated her apple-plump cheeks in thick Vaseline. The most charming southern drawl dripped from her lips, making you think she was proper, but then she'd flash you a fiery smirk and you'd know she was feisty. Oh, was she feisty. She walked around in a transparent, cotton nightgown with nothing underneath, hosting all sorts of people in her home this way, feigning innocence. Always a tomboy, she was a champion tennis player and different from anyone I knew. Most of all, she loved her Lord. She was glorious.

Then there is my maternal grandmother, Joyce. She is artistic and adventurous. She has a smirk, too, which lets on that we are going to have a bit of fun. On a whim, she would orchestrate elaborate tea parties for us, with mandatory wide-brimmed hats, where everyone spoke in an English accent and flung their pinky fingers to the sky. Her living room is filled with art books and oil paintings. She is a masterpiece.

Aunt Lucy—who inspired me to keep having children until I had a daughter I could name after her—took me and my cousin skinny-dipping when we were ten years old. While we swam, she laughed and hooted from the shore. She hosted grand parties where she would don her wedding dress, faded with time. Her mother died in her home where she was hosting a church social, and Aunt Lucy managed to keep the party going while sneaking the body out the back to the hearse. Every person who came to her house, day or night, she'd let in for some simple hospitality and connection. This usually meant sandwiches and swaying around the house to the tunes of Duke Ellington. She was a gift.

These women. I often wonder if they, too, heard those whispers, "Too much. Too much." If they did, they managed to free themselves in spite of it: elaborate gestures of drama, silly runs to the beach, surfing and dancing, wearing nightgowns well into the late afternoon. And they still loved God. They still loved their families. I was entranced by their radiance and decided that I didn't want to be like my mom, caged and empty; I wanted to be free too.

I didn't see my mom free until she turned fifty, and it makes me want to beat the earth and wail that it took so long.

ON THE ROAD

My childhood on the road could be described with the sights and smells of a midwestern gas station: Indian artifacts, roadside attractions, and threadbare diners with that greasy smell. I remember seeing a mummy for a dollar once when I went to pee, sifting through arrowheads as I waited for Mom to pay for our gas, and the thrill of picking out a single Atomic Fireball for five cents as a rare treat.

There's a story my mama fondly tells about how one night she breast-fed me while steering our motor home up a mountain pass and towing a concrete pump behind it in a blizzard. Nearly everyone who hears her tell about it shudders, but Mama always has a twinkle in her eye when she recites the story. She had adventure in her bones.

Dad built monolithic concrete domes for homes and commercial use, working for himself most of the time. No matter how magnificent they were, he was stressed about them. Dad was brilliant, but he was not good at business. We would have starved to death if it weren't for our grandparents sending checks when we had nothing. Sometimes we traveled the country with him, and sometimes he went alone while we stayed in my grandparents' home back in Charleston. When we traveled with Dad we slept wherever my parents could stash us.

We lived in a yellow Bronco when I was tiny and new. We lived in a barn with an outhouse so far away we ended up peeing in the woods. We lived in dirty motel rooms, befriending the maids. And sometimes, when we were lucky, we lived in apartments with indoor bathrooms and something more than a cooler and a camping stove for a kitchen.

When I was four, we lived in a semitruck container. Dad rigged up a bed high off the floor where he hung a mattress for him and Mama to sleep on. My sister Katie Beth and I slept under it. Mama cooked on an outdoor stove, and we used the job site's port-a-john.

One afternoon on that project, Dad caught a six-foot king snake all shiny and slick. He put us all safely in his truck so he could show it to us. While draping the snake over his shoulder, he suddenly dropped it, and it quickly slithered under the truck and into the engine. We all ran screaming from the truck, like ants scattering when their nest is kicked. It was at this job site that I have a sweet, vivid memory of my dad helping me build things with my hands in the leftover concrete.

Once our family of six slept in a thirteen-foot trailer in the Florida Everglades during alligator mating season. Every night we lay in bed and heard the loud bellows all around us. My sisters and I had to take a class on how to zigzag your way away from the eight-foot alligators sauntering around the playground like they owned the place. Our trailer was so tiny we had to store things in the small bathroom and use the bathhouse a short walk from our place. Our homeschool books were stacked on the toilet, and my beloved pawn shop violin was tenderly placed in the shower. One morning, our water backed up and I found my violin floating in dirty, brown water. I laid it the hot sun to dry and was thrilled that it still played, even after its bath. Every night when we had to pee, we'd have to wake a sister to tiptoe to the bathroom, glancing around with our flashlight for the glinty eyes of a gator ready to pounce.

Every place we lived, Mama made it special and homey. Flowers, furniture from the side of the road, and dishes from the local thrift shops filled whatever space we were allotted. A few weeks or months later, she would take everything down and give it to people who needed it, and we would move on. I don't recall her ever complaining about where we lived. She always made things beautiful.

Wherever we lived, when the circus came to town, Dad was always there at first dawn to help the troupe hoist up the giant red and white tent. He was a friendly guy and was fascinated with the knots they used to raise the tent. It wasn't work to him; it was a dream come true. That night we would all get to go for free, popcorn included. Throughout the performances, Dad would spend the night waving and smiling at his new friends, and I felt we were the luckiest people there.

When I was about eight years old, my grandmother Joyce flew to Oregon to help Mama drive back across the country with us. Just a few days into our trip, we were trying to make it up a big mountain pass in Colorado Springs before a blizzard hit. In our Aerostar van was Mama, my grandmother Joyce, two sisters, a baby, me, and a cat. We were creeping up the mountain and it was already snowing hard. Mama decided to try a shortcut to get up faster. I was engrossed in a book when all of a sudden we were spinning, and we tipped up on the side of our van, spilling the baby and the kitty litter and my book all over. Mama climbed out and saw that we had fallen against the only snow bank in sight. On either side were thousands of feet of nothing but steep drop-offs. It was freezing, and of course there was no cell phone. We all huddled together and prayed for a miracle, and before we had time to say "Amen," we saw five Hispanic men walking toward us through the white sheet of snow. They wordlessly picked up our van off its side and turned it to face back down the mountain, then left without a word. Mama said they didn't leave footprints.

Cross-country trips were always exciting. We would take the middle seat out of our van and layer the floor with blankets so it was like a giant mattress. To this day, there is no sound more soothing to me than the whir of wheels under my head. We would sleep there, but we would also do flips, and I would stand on my head as we flew down the highway. Babies would sleep in a bucket car seat, but it wouldn't be buckled in most of the time. This provided easy access for Mama to breast-feed while she drove. Late at night, I would wait for the girls to fall asleep and I would crawl up between my parents. I'd sit on my knees, elbows on each arm rest, leaning forward into the soothing adult talk. Sometimes they would play games with me, like "Guess who I am thinking of?" or finding all the letters of the alphabet on the signs that flew by us in the night. It felt so glorious to feel special and grown-up like that. Dad was notorious for falling asleep anywhere, including while he drove, so I took it upon myself to keep him awake and our family safe. I would spend hours watching him, pinching him every time I saw his head bow. Since I was awake way past my bedtime, I would also nod off until we reached a cheap motel to crash in. When we'd finally pull over, I would wait eagerly as my dad negotiated the cheapest price. Sometimes we would go to several places to find it, often looping back to the first. Dad would carry me in, and I would finally fall into a deep sleep.

We listened to old, dusty cassette tapes of the band Asleep at the Wheel as we crossed state lines, blowing kisses all around to celebrate. Sometimes Dad would pull out his harmonica and play soulful bluegrass tunes while he drove with his knees. I vividly remember driving in the middle of nowhere, surrounded by corn fields, with not a light or an establishment in sight. We were almost out of gas when our parents woke us all up. It was the middle of the night, and they asked us to pray with them that we wouldn't get stranded. We watched the gas gauge needle as each one of us prayed with all our being. Prayer by prayer, that needle started rising till our tank was a quarter full, and we knew we could make it to a gas station.

Being on the road drew our family together. There was no one to impress and no one to keep up with. Adventure filled us up to the brim, giving all of us an insatiable taste for it.

ISLAND ADVENTURE

One of the greatest adventures of my childhood was when my dad got a building project in the Canary Islands, off the coast of Morocco. To prepare us for the flight, my grandmother sewed all of us girls, including my mom, matching blue and white dresses. We looked just like the von Trapp family. The idea was that if a girl got lost, my mom could point to one of us to show people what they were looking for, since we all looked alike.

This was my very first plane ride. The flight attendants spoiled us with things that we were never allowed: kids meals all to ourselves with prizes and soft drinks and a movie that wasn't rated G. *Mrs Doubtfire* was a far cry away from *Little House on the Prairie*, which we only watched as a special treat at home. Sitting in that row with my family, squirmy baby Georgia Ann on my mother's lap, I felt so happy. So very, very happy.

After nearly twenty-four hours of travel, we arrived at the small island on a tiny, unstable airplane. We were all exhausted and ravenously hungry, so we lugged our suitcases, which were packed full of grits and peanut butter, to the only restaurant nearby.

In our family, we had certain foods we always ate. We ate chicken only once or twice a week, we ate a lot of ramen noodles, and we did not eat eggs. In fact, we would all gag at the sight of them. The restaurant menu was all in Spanish, and we couldn't understand anything, except for one word. Tortilla. When the waiter came to take our order, we told him we wanted a tortilla and cheese—a quesadilla.

"Okay, egg and cheese," he said in his broken English.

"No. Tortilla. Cheese. No egg."

"Okay. Egg and cheese."

"No egg. Just cheese."

The cook came out to try to translate for us in his broken English. Finally they seemed to understand and went back to prepare it. When they returned, they brought us an omelet with cheese over potatoes. In desperation, we timidly took tiny bites of the strange concoction, and before we knew what was happening we were staring at empty plates. This was our first experience in a country where we couldn't speak the language. When we returned home months later, we discovered that tortilla was a type of omelet in Spain. "Egg and cheese, no egg."

Throughout this trip my family lived in a small apartment on the eighth floor of a high-rise. Everything inside was square and plain, but we had a beautiful balcony overlooking the street. We could even see a sliver of ocean on the horizon. Because we didn't have air conditioning, we pulled one of the mattresses out onto the balcony, and that is where my parents slept. At night we would all curl up together and read for hours on that mattress, with the sounds of the street and the breeze off the ocean wrapping us up in warmth.

Every day when Dad came home from working, four little blond heads would be sticking out over the balcony watching for him. As he started up the elevator we would run to greet him at the top. I loved how he smelled like concrete dust when he returned home, and I loved being there to greet him every day, which was a rare treat. One day we decided to just have one girl out there to surprise him when the elevator doors popped open. The next day we switched, and it became a guessing game for Dad which girl or combo of girls would be there when the elevator doors opened up. One evening Mom was making dinner, and a misshapen carrot, resembling an obese sunbather, made us all laugh till we cried. We decided to draw a face on it and set it outside the elevator to surprise Dad. The howling was contagious as we all jumped up and down at Dad's reaction. This became our game, and it was ever so much fun. Dolls and misshapen vegetables and handstands gave us something to look forward to in the evenings when Dad came home; it all made for the simplest source of joy in that time of our lives.

What was not so fun was the language barrier. No one spoke English on the island, and the Spanish dictionary we packed was completely worthless since the Spanish there was mixed with an African language. The island was sandwiched between Spain and Morocco and invited a blend of dialects. Though the island was warm and beautiful, people there were cold. Brutally unfriendly. We had come from the South, the land of sickly sweet gentility, where everyone greeted each other warmly, like they were family, in singsong voices that wafted into the equally warm air. No matter what we did on this Canary Island, we could not seem to make friends. We only had each other. My sisters and I played with sponges and dolls we found at the flea market, and we read to pass the days. Whenever we walked to the supermarket, we were greeted by cold, hard stares. We struggled to communicate our basic needs, and they mocked us as we butchered what little Spanish we knew in our southern drawl. We didn't eat meat for months because my mom just couldn't figure out how to tell them we wanted the chicken without the head on it. Making the employees at the supermarket smile became a game for our family. We would draw them pictures and learn their names. Finally, weeks later, they started opening their hearts, and we received bread and meat samples aplenty—and a chicken without a head.

Then there was that time when all we could afford to eat was lentils and hard white bread because my parents had lost the bank card and we had to wait weeks for another to be shipped from the United States.

Whenever we could, we would take a bus to the beach. What a sight that must have been, all five of us pouring into the bus, clutching our beach stuff. The sand was white and the water was crystal blue. The shores were crowded with people from every country you could imagine, but none of them spoke English. The women went topless; this was a major shock to our sheltered Christian eyes. My mother was so horrified she made Dad surf on the rocky shores instead of ever going to a beach again. On one beach trip with just us girls, Mom was distracted and didn't see my baby sister, who was still nursing at the time, crawling over to a beautiful, topless black woman. Just before she latched on, my mom screamed and picked her up in a swoop. We always joked that Georgia Ann just wanted a little chocolate milk that day.

One sunny day, my mom lined us all up on the beach and told us not to move, that she wanted to swim for a bit. I wrapped my arms around baby Georgia to keep her from sampling other womens' breast milk, and my mother put on her snorkel and paddled out so far that we could barely see her. When she was snorkeling she saw a giant purple sea urchin down on the sea floor and knew that we would love seeing it. She was always one for making everyday life educational, so she scooped it up with a shovel and was walking it back to us when it tipped over and jammed one of its needles under her thumbnail. Instantly, she was flooded with nausea and felt faint. She started asking people around us if it was poisonous but no one understood what she was asking, so she told me I had to be brave and watch the girls, never letting them go into the water or out of my sight. I was seven and they were five, four, and one. We were in a foreign country. She walked away in her bikini, searching deliriously for a hospital. She finally found one and was met with flirtation and laughter instead of concern, so she assumed she wasn't about to die and returned back to us huddled on the beach.

A few weeks later, baby Georgia Ann was napping on the balcony and Mom was running up and down the stairs for exercise. All of us big girls came out of the hot apartment to watch her run, and as we came out the door closed and locked behind us. Mama's heart just about stopped when she finished her exercises and discovered what had happened. Though she was bone tired, she left us again, the three of us crouched in the doorway, and ran five miles to Dad's job site to get a key. The whole way she was praying to God that the baby wouldn't wake up and hurt herself or, worse, fall off the balcony. When our heroine mother returned home, sweaty and breathless, we opened the door to find our golden-haired baby sleeping peacefully right where we had left her.

That lonely time on the island brought us close together as a family. On the weekends, when Dad could get away, we would pile into our tiny, white, tin can of a car and head to a rural, non-topless beach to camp. I have the clearest memories of staying up late to see the stars come out and eating potatoes boiled in seawater while we told stories around the fire. We would play all day, Dad would surf the rocky coastline, and we would all fall asleep to the ocean's roar in one big pile of arms and legs. One time the tide came up so high it threatened to wash our tent away. My valiant mother spent the entire night building a wall so she wouldn't have to wake us to move our whole campsite back. Mama was a relentless protector of her family. Dad snored away the whole ordeal, oblivious to the threat.

We stayed a year on the island, and we left with buckets full of memories. On the flight home, it was just going to be us girls and an eighteen-year-old Mormon boy from Utah who worked with my dad. Dad had to stay back to finish the job and he wanted someone to go with us to help out. Mama was bustling around trying to get everything packed up and ready, and she kept asking Dad if he had the passports. "Yes," he kept assuring her. As we boarded our first flight home on the toy-like airplane, Mama asked for the passports. Dad's eyes grew wide—he had left them back at the apartment. I remember him yelling encouragingly across the gate separating us, "Don't worry! Just say the Pledge of Allegiance in your southern accent, and they'll let you in for sure. Plus, you just look American!" And so we took off from the Canary Islands not knowing what would await us on our layover in Spain. As soon as we landed, we found out the only chance we had of making our next flight was to go to the American embassy and apply for temporary passports. We bolted. Left all of our luggage in the middle of the airport in a great big pile and grabbed a taxi to the embassy—one woman, three identically dressed girls, a nursing baby, and a eighteen-year-old boy who was holding on for dear life. We only had a small amount of cash and were terrified it wouldn't be enough for a taxi ride back, much less enough if we had to stay in Madrid.

When we got to the embassy, we were sternly questioned. "How do we know these are your children?" the officer asked.

"Um, I'll breast-feed one of them if you want," replied my mother.

We were all obviously from the same family—except for the teenage boy—all blond, all in our blue and white dresses. We looked like cloned copies. Minutes before our plane was about to take off, they gave us five temporary passports and we raced back to the airport to grab our bags, which had miraculously not been touched, and boarded, exhausted. We returned home to Charleston safe and sound, and we didn't even need to say the Pledge of Allegiance.

CHARLESTON

When we weren't on the road, we lived in Charleston, in a big, brick Colonial house owned by my grandparents. The lavish home was a stark contrast to our road life, but it brought wonderful familiarity that I craved as a child. In between traveling, I spent my days there running barefoot beneath the romantic Spanish moss, fishing, riding my bike, and visiting the elderly neighbors. There was Miss Mary, with the palest skin I had ever seen, ink-black hair, and swollen arthritic fingers that played "Fur Elise" on the piano so gracefully. There was Uncle Art, who brought us brown paper bags of salty, boiled peanuts. We would go across the street to visit him and his wife, Betty, and play on his rope swing and stick our feet in the lake to let the minnows nibble our toes. There was Miss Jan, who had a wishing well and a shiny, black, old-fashioned joggling board; and Miss Lucille, who had a secret garden behind an overgrown brick wall back behind her house. She made me warm sourdough bread with butter melted on it, and we would watch Jeopardy in the evenings sometimes. I have a thousand small memories of the glorious childhood I had there. It was an anchor for my soul.

Charleston also meant bows in my hair, frilly socks, and tight patent leather shoes. It brought expectations and restrictions. It brought feelings of not belonging. Half of my life was spent wild on the road, and the other half was spent keeping up with the Joneses. My mother was different in Charleston, rarely present and often crying.

Every year when Easter approached, my sisters and I would be dragged all over town to try on new white shoes. We had to look perfect to go to the egg hunt and especially to go to church on Sunday. Egg hunts in Charleston were grand: ponies and baby ducks and bunnies and children done up in their finest smocked garb. I often had tiny burns on my earlobes where the curling iron had set my hair just right. My sisters and I were an attraction—little ladies with excellent manners all standing in a row. We craved approval, and the result was the very best behaved children. We didn't know we had any other choice.

Despite the underlying turmoil of trying to be good enough, I have wonderful mental snapshots of living there: playing in the attic for hours with my sisters, picnicking on the beach with my Aunt Kathy, trying to make perfume with the nectar of the honeysuckles surrounding my house, fishing with my neighbor Tom and catching more fish than him, putting on circuses and charging admission, playing a game called Giants with my favorite cousin, Kathrine, and sisters, Thanksgiving dinners bursting with food and family, Vivaldi wafting through the air, and walking through the neighborhood to my Aunt Lucy's carol sing. The much anticipated carol sing was a huge party held on Aunt Lucy and Uncle Quaddy's wedding anniversary every year. We would sit by the piano and sing, drink hot apple cider, eat old-fashioned cookies, and watch movies on the second floor while the adults carried on downstairs. Sometimes Aunt Lucy would wear her wedding gown with its champagne train trailing off of the piano, where she would sit singing "Silent Night."

Charleston was rich with family. I had so many cousins; there were more than twenty of us altogether on my dad's side. Every family event was teeming with mischief and fun. We had hot dog roasts on the beach under the full moon, and we would play hide and seek in the shadowed sand dunes. We put on plays and filled long, elaborately decorated tables with laughter.

My sisters and I would spend our summers on Sullivan's Island in front of my grandparents' house, surfing, swimming, building forts out of sand. My legs would burn as I lay on my belly with Kathrine, finding periwinkles that popped up in the sand. I would run back up to the house to devour whatever food my mom had prepared and run right back out. I owned more bathing suits than clothes. I skinny-dipped the second the sun started sinking and fell asleep on a mattress we dragged onto the porch. The sounds of the waves and the frogs lulled me to sleep with my sisters' warm legs tangled around mine.

CAMP

Every summer the lush, green mountains of western North Carolina are flooded with camp people. Moms and dads with tanned skin, perfect ponytails, and white teeth. Their brand-new, name-brand outdoor clothes are fresh with creases from the package. They fill bakeries and swimming holes with fresh wonder and giggle over iced lattes. And then there are the other camp people. They show up to the local hot dog joint in long denim skirts and dirty white tennis shoes. The women have thin, straggly hair to their waists. They wear baggy T-shirts with Christian symbols printed on them. They aren't smiling. Their husband and kids aren't smiling. They aren't smiling because they have just finished up at the church camp I attended as a child. They aren't smiling because guilt and shame have been beaten into them all week with short breaks for playing field games or painting ceramics, and they are returning home to a similar life void of joy and full of striving. I want to rescue them and tell them they're wrong. I want to tell them of a deep, free love that cannot be earned.

If you were to ask someone about their memories of camp, I bet they would include late nights in the woods, laughing around the campfire, swimming, being free. I have fond memories of camp too— getting away from the confusion of home life, being responsible for only myself, not having to be a big sister or dutiful daughter. The fact that I could buy candy with my twenty dollars in spending money was enough to make me love it.

If I were to sum up the camp I attended in one sweeping statement, it would be *hiding my body*. The grown-ups around me cared more about what I wore than they did about my heart. My shirts weren't baggy enough over my undeveloped breasts, or my shorts skirted the top of my knees, so I was a problem. No one saw that I was hurting.

We swam, separated from the boys, in modest one-piece suits underneath layers of clothes. One time a boy splashed me on our way to lunch and my billowing T-shirt got slightly wet, showing the outline of my bathing suit, which covered my barely there breasts. I was sent back to my cabin to change and missed lunch because a boy could have seen that I was a girl, and I would have caused that boy to struggle with sexual feelings for the rest of his life. We girls carried such great responsibility.

When the sun was on its way to setting, we were made to put on skirts to attend evening chapel. I felt so feminine in my skirt, my chastity alluring the boys like moths to a flame.

The year we were ten, my cousin Kathrine and I, who were used to scampering on the beach at Sullivan's Island wearing barely anything, were running around the cabin before bed, giggling and naked as jaybirds. Our beautiful young counselor took us aside and sat us down. Soberly, she told us how much God was grieved with our actions. She proceeded to tell us that she was so modest she showered with washcloths covering her body so God wouldn't see her.

I stifled a laugh and thought to myself, "Lady, I don't know if you know this, but God actually *made* your body."

There was more spiritual shame. I remember being made to sign a promise in the front of my Bible.

I, Helen Joy Paul, promise to God that I will never:

- Drink alcohol
- Smoke
- Have sex before marriage

I didn't even know what sex was, really. It would take years after I was married for me to untangle the damage done through the shame heaped on me there.

Our evenings were full of long altar calls while the neighboring camps were playing hide and seek with fireflies. One evening, I looked up after daydreaming with my head down in prayer position, lulled into a trance by the repeat chorus of "Just as I am." There were just a few of us left in the audience; the only ones without sin to confess. I finally raised my hand, mostly so they would stop the altar call. I was escorted outside to an adult who waited with pity in her eyes for the sin that was to come out of my mouth.

"I guess I gossip sometimes," I said quietly, mostly because I didn't believe it to be true.

You would have thought I had said I had killed someone, what with the dramatic praying and moaning that occurred after my confession, leading me to lie prostrate on the ground and beg for forgiveness. God must have been so sad looking down at me, His precious child. He already forgave me long before I asked. I could have whispered it in a rainstorm, and He would have heard me. I just wanted to go outside and play our nighttime game, I just wanted to enjoy my few days there.

At night in my bunk bed, the words of the preachers and the Bible verses taken out of context swirled inside my head, and I whispered different versions of the Sinner's Prayer into the muggy darkness. I didn't know if I was saying it right.

Things at home were not as severe, but still, damaging threads of "truth" penetrated my heart. Every man and boy was picturing me naked, and it was my responsibility to protect them. Even more damaging was the thought that God was harsh and void of joy and that He could be manipulated by this little girl at camp saying just the right words in exactly the right way.

CALIFORNIA

My childhood felt like waves in the ocean; nothing was consistent, everything ebbed and flowed. There were days of glory and days of confusion, but nestled in the chaos was a time that I treasure, a small nest egg of feeling connected as a family, of feeling planted, of feeling sure. Oh, California, the love poem of my childhood.

The only constant in my young life, other than my mother reading to me every night, was that my family would come home from whatever job Dad was doing to spend Christmas in my grandparents' beautiful Colonial home in Charleston. We held onto every tiny Christmas tradition with white knuckles, shoving every memory that we could into our hearts like we were starving.

The fall I turned eleven, we packed up our trusty Aerostar van and started to drive up towards Chicago. Dad had accepted this job with the condition that it would include a place for his family to stay. We were eager to get there and set up house, and we spent the last few hours of the trip singing and laughing. Hope filled us up. We arrived at a dark hotel and spent the night. Early the next morning we drove to what was to be our home for the next few months and found that it was nothing more than a barn. It had no heat, electricity, or plumbing, and chickens were incubating in it. That was the day I first saw Dad cry. I ran my fingers through his greasy hair as he hunched over the bed on his knees, his worn hands covering his face. My parents told us they were sorry, and since we couldn't start the job there without a place to live, we were going to head west to start another job in Northern California. When they said we wouldn't be able to make it home for Christmas, we all wept. I closed my eyes and imagined the milky-white nativity my mother had made and the way I would stare at the gifts the wise men brought. I thought of the carol-sing party I would miss with my cousins and the nativity play we put on every year—towels and blankets on our heads and angel wings on the babies.

Heavyhearted, we loaded back up into our van and headed west to the unknown, the setting sun illuminating our tear-stained cheeks. Days later we arrived at a remote mountain lot surrounded by trees hundreds of feet tall, and right next to the job site was a twenty-seven-foot trailer just for us. It ended up being the coziest, most love-filled home that we would ever share.

The trailer was so small that our chores were done in minutes and we had endless time for exploring and creating. Mama and Dad slept on the pullout couch. There were four of us girls at the time, and we all slept in the back bedroom, where there was one bed. Every night we rotated which two would get to sleep in the bed. Floor, bed, bed, floor. Repeat. It was always exciting when you got to sleep in the bed twice in a row!

We had never been with our father as much as we were there. We took him lunch and went to "help" him tie steel. We spent the days homeschooling and reading long chapter books while Mama stroked our hair. We piled on top of each other, munching popcorn, and knitted tiny, crooked scarves.

It snowed constantly, and at night the snow would fall from the branches high above and hit our roof. It sounded like we were being bombed, but we grew used to it. Our hot water lasted less than a minute, so showers had to be spaced hours apart, and you had to turn it off and on to get all the soap rinsed out. Every two weeks we would drive to a hotel down the mountain and spend the weekend swimming in the heated pool and taking all the hot showers we wanted.

Preparing for Christmas that year was holy. We cut down a small, scraggly sapling from outside and decorated it with ornaments we glued, stitched, and fashioned from flour and salt. While Mama read to us, we worked on Christmas gifts for each other—doll clothes and cross-stitched treasures. We went to the small town down the mountain and attended their old-fashioned Christmas, roasting chestnuts by a fire, and taking a sleigh ride. I remember stepping into a bookstore and finding a book about gymnastics stacked on one of the shelves. I ran my fingers over the glossy images of tumbling and flying high over the uneven bars. "One day," I promised myself as I set it back on the shelf and returned to the snowy streets for carols by the roaring fire. There were a hundred precious memories that Advent season, but greatest of all was that we were together, present in a way we had never experienced. The ache in our hearts for our home back east grew so faint we couldn't feel it.

Christmas morning, I woke up excited to give my handmade gifts to my sisters and parents. I walked out of the bedroom, and laid out on the couch was the gymnastics book, a shiny blue leotard, and a note saying that they had signed me up for three gymnastics lessons. Everyone else had thrift-store dolls and handmade blankets, and the whole family looked at me with shining faces. The little bit of money we had had been spent to surprise me. That's what I love about my family. It's never about fairness; it's always about giving. Later that morning, I found another present wrapped under the tree. It was a dark green, leather diary with a lock on it and my name embossed in gold across the front cover. After opening our gifts we went sledding outside, laughing and running around pink-cheeked. That was the most wonderful Christmas I had growing up.

That Christmas stored up a lifetime of happy memories for me, more than a dozen Christmases spent in our big southern home would have. I would end up needing these memories, because two years later my father would pick up a nail gun, splintering our family into pieces.

BABY DOLL

After the initial shock from Dad's suicide attempt had settled, it was apparent that Mom would need to stay at the hospital for an extended time. Since she had been homeschooling us, the small Christian school associated with our church offered to let us come for the rest of the year. This was a bright light in the bleak darkness of uncertainty—a break from the sadness, a break from the adult responsibilities—and it felt indulgent. I loved school. I loved taking notes and taking tests. I loved lunchtime. I loved being around other kids. At home I'd have to pack lunches, get up in the night when my one-year-old sister would cry, and do other motherly things, but at school I could be simple and childlike. I let the other girls take me under their wing, I carried a doll and fed her when I ate, I wore pigtails nearly every day. I didn't have to act innocent, because I was. Thirteen years at home, and I was clueless about anything not related to *Little House on the Prairie*. On my class trip I lost two teeth and pretended I believed in the tooth fairy. All the girls in my class gathered their change and put it under my pillow, much to my delight.

It could have been so different. I could have been mocked and tortured, but instead I was adored and mothered. I'm sure that I was annoying and needy, but I was never made to feel that way. My mother wasn't there, but I had a class full of girls to take care of me.

I remember waking up early with butterflies in my stomach and sneaking to the hiding place under the sink I shared with my sisters, where I had put a treasured bottle of Bath and Body Works plumeria-scented body spray. I would spritz myself and think of Matt, my very first crush. Matt was the bad boy of our class. He was always getting in trouble and giving me intense looks through his shaggy blond hair. I wanted to make him good. I wanted to save him. Every time he had to go to the principal's office, I would place a sticker on the top of his desk, and by the end of the school year the desk was covered.

A month or so after starting school, a decision was made that instead of living with my grandparents and my sisters I would go and live with Kathrine's family. She was the same age and in my class and this was a dream come true. Suddenly, I wasn't someone's big sister; I was only responsible for myself. I pushed down the guilt of leaving my sisters at the worst time of our lives and allowed myself to be cared for. My aunt rubbed my back at night and brought me hot chocolate in the morning. The pain of what was happening at the hospital with Dad was dulled by the whir of normal living—uniforms and homework, dinners around the table, and adventures till dark. I look back on my life, and I see an ocean of painful, hard things, but this break saved me. It gave me breath until the next wave.

A year passed, and I felt like I was emerging from a tornado. Right when I thought I was living a normal life, when Dad was home from the hospital and had started walking again I was yanked from my aunt's home and moved to Hendersonville, North Carolina, where my mom's family was. It was messy, and it broke my heart almost as much as my dad's suicide attempt did. I was weeks away from starting high school. I was going to be a cheerleader and had tryouts in a week. I had already bought my green, plaid skirts and my knee-high socks.

One day before we left for North Carolina, I wrote a dramatic note about how I couldn't live anymore if I had to go, left it for my mom, and peddled my bike miles and miles down the beach to a small grocery store when I realized I had no plan for what to do next. While I waited in a corner of the parking lot, I saw three police cars rushing in the direction of my house, leaving a trail of wailing sirens behind them.

Oh my gosh, they've called the police, I thought. I'm in so much trouble.

Part of me was thrilled to be the star in such a dramatic story, but mostly I knew I was going to be in the biggest trouble of my life. I finally decided to head back. When I got home and opened the door to the kitchen, head hung low, there was my mother, cooking. "Hey, haven't seen you in a while."

I wasn't even missed.

NOAH

I met my husband when I was fourteen, after my father's secrets had poured out. My family had moved to North Carolina to live with my mother's parents. While we waited for my grandparents to find a house, we all stayed in a motor home in the campground of the Presbyterian conference center that I had grown up going to every summer.

I saw him from across the pool. He was nineteen, big and manly. His hair was curly and stuck out in a kinky fro. His olive skin was tanned from the summer. More than what he looked like, I was drawn to him bending down and inviting kids of all ages to come play sharks and minnows. I watched as he gathered everyone, and I knew I wanted to marry him.

The first time he remembers meeting me, I was wearing overalls. He saw me from afar and told his brother, "See that girl? I'm going to marry her."

His father had supported my grandfather on the mission field back in the '70s, and one day they ran into each other and our families were finally introduced. His name was Noah.

That was a summer of heartache for both of us. His mother had left his father out of the blue, right when Noah was finishing high school, and his parents were getting divorced that summer. Even after more than a year of caregiving for my father, my mother was holding onto threads, trying to will Dad to live, to stay. Every day he tried to leave her, leave us.

Our families started doing everything together—me, my sisters, Noah, and his older brother, Eric. The first time we hung out, they invited us over to their house to watch the new *Anne of Green Gables* since we didn't have TV. I sat across the couch from Noah and could barely watch the movie, I was so in love with him.

After a summer of camping, swimming, and eating together, I was more sure than ever that I would marry him. I called him "big brother," and he scooped my sisters and me into bear hugs of love.

The second we moved in with my grandparents, my mother collapsed into bed, defeated from more than a year of tirelessly taking care of my father. Dad had been sent to rehab for an addiction that he had admitted to after his injury. As summer faded into fall, it was time for Noah to return to his second year of college in South Carolina. I found the thought unbearable. Right before he was to leave, he made the decision to stay back a semester and go to the local community college so he could be there for our family. That fall he drove me to school several days a week, he paid for our family to visit Dad with money he made with a start-up internet company, and he surprised us with tickets to the movies. Best of all, he loved us all deeply. I barely felt the sting of Mom's depression, because Noah stepped in.

Eventually, Dad left Mom. After so many years of emptying herself out for him, she finally let him go. The details of their separation are blurry but, physically and emotionally damaged and at the mental age of someone in elementary school, Dad moved into our old motorhome and attempted to live his life apart from us.

Our first Thanksgiving in North Carolina, Noah and I combined our families at one long table, a ragtag bunch of brokenhearted people. It felt like home. Joy was abundant in the midst of horrible pain.

That fall I started writing love letters to Noah every day, but instead of mailing them to him, I put them in a box under my bed. When I was around him I was his little sister, but alone in my room I knew, beyond the shadow of a doubt, that I would marry him one day. As the box filled, I decided I would give it to him on our wedding day.

That Christmas Noah bought us all matching pajamas. Blue stripes with red around the edges. We watched movies and played in the snow. He and Eric made it one of the best Christmases we had ever had.

When Noah went back to college, my heart ached. He came home on many weekends and breaks but talked about a girl he liked. I strained to put on my little-sister act. I would close my eyes and fantasize about him coming home and rescuing me. About how he would take me away from the chaos and hurt of my family and we would make a new life.

The following summer, I was volunteering at a camp for adults with special needs and had free time after all the campers were in bed. Noah lived with his dad in the residential part of the conference center where it was held, and he would just happen to stroll by at just the right time so we could take a walk together. One night we sat on the porch of the old hotel on campus, and he told me, "I'm pretty sure I'm going to marry you. You're too young now, but I will wait for you." I assured him that I felt the same way. He held my hand. I was fifteen, and he was twenty.

Soon after, Noah started dating someone else. She was his first official girlfriend. I was crushed and confused. That summer, his brother graduated from the small Christian school we both went to. Eric was my very best friend at school. I cheered for his basketball team, we were leads in the play, and we took band trips together. When Noah hurt me with his betrayal, I found myself holding hands with his brother in a movie one late night. For two weeks we had a whirlwind romance—picnics, poetry, and lots of kisses. Somewhere along the way Noah broke up with his girlfriend, and I found myself in another dark movie theatre where both brothers simultaneously reached for my hand. The next day I told Eric I couldn't date him because I wanted to marry his brother.

That fall, on my sixteenth birthday, Noah told my mom he wanted to marry me, but that he would wait. She was blindsided and confused by our big-brother/little-sister act. I listened from my room as they talked. She wanted me to go to college. He told her that I would and that he would move across the world if he needed to so I could finish college. He gave me a red knit sweater that year and a Nickel Creek CD with a song, "When you come back down." I lay in my bed with those lyrics on repeat, clutching my red sweater, and I exhaled with relief that he would finally be mine.

The following summer, Noah was newly twenty-one and had his first beer one sticky summer evening. I remember it because he came by camp when I had free time, and we took a walk. He put his mouth on mine, and I could smell the hops. Then he took me to the driveway of his childhood home to look at the stars and slipped a small key ring onto my finger, a promise.

HIGH SCHOOL

Our red cheerleading skirts had to hit our knees. Three years prior, they had to be over the knee, but as the years moved on, the hem allowance would inch up just a bit higher. I guess they figured out kneecaps didn't automatically throw young men into a life of sin.

I adored cheerleading; it was a time when my "too-muchness" was in my favor. Often when I showed up to the basketball game none of the other cheerleaders would be there, so I would jump around with the enthusiasm of ten girls, choreographing my own impromptu halftime show, complete with gymnastics. People loved me, and I drank up their adoration like someone who had just been rescued from the desert. I felt seen.

Once at an away game, Noah had come to watch his brother play basketball. I couldn't wait to feel his adoring gaze on me as I cheered, but every time I went to perform he would turn away from me. Through the crowd of people who saw me, I saw his back and felt his rejection. Was I too much for him too?

High school was such a relief for me, an escape from the hard things in my life. My sisters were still homeschooled, and I was the only one who attended the small, local Christian school for two years.

I was different from the other girls at school. I wore orange pants and brought hummus in my lunch long before hummus was cool. I had many good friends, but I still felt separate. My head was full of Noah and plans for marriage and escaping my home life. My moral compass was mountain strong. I was armed to face the world with all the things I was doing right. I went into mourning every time I heard a friend had sex, because I just couldn't understand it.

Strong language and bullying were a shock to my system. I agonized when I saw teachers being disrespected. I sat aside in the corner when classmates would cheat, which was every day. (My geometry teacher was legally blind, and all it took to get a 100 on his tests was to glance over at his answer key.) My chemistry teacher, a smart woman with a PhD, got so frustrated with the rowdiness of the boys in my class just two weeks into the school year that she stacked up all the tests for the year and set the answer keys beside them. "If you copy the answers, you get 100," she huffed as she sat down, crushed. I dutifully copied a little every day. At the end of the year, many students had not done it, so she gave extra credit so the class wouldn't fail. I did the extra credit too, and ended up with a 130 in chemistry and certificates of honor. I wouldn't know about anything but H2O when I went to college.

I rode to school every morning with Eric. Even though I was in love with Noah, I still was drawn to his brother. I wrote him a note every day and slipped it through the cracks in his locker. He wrote me one about once a week. My junior year we performed the leads of Daddy Warbucks and Orphan Annie for the school play. We did everything together.

My innocence intrigued my classmates, and they had fun teaching me things. Once in history class, someone told me to ask our teacher—an elderly ex-missionary who was home from serving God elsewhere—what an orgasm was. I did, and I instantly regretted it. I will never forget the flush on his face. Sometimes my naivete got the better of me.

Despite the separateness I felt, in a high school that was so small we were all close, playing every sport and doing all of the fine arts. Almost everyone played in the band in the morning. I played violin alongside the brass and the flutes. Sports practices and games were spaced evenly so that we could sing in the choir or perform in the school play as well. We would come in from soccer, shed our dirty cleats in the gym, and jump right into play practice. Living day in and day out with these people made them family to me.

The kids in this school were a blend of dutiful Christians raised under the thumb of legalism and rebellious kids who had been expelled from public schools. Then there were the ones who were in between. Kids who would leave the chapel service, where a riveting sermon about saving sex for marriage had just been preached, and load into an old van where the girls without boyfriends gave blow jobs to boys who took what they wanted.

During high school, for the first time in my life I had my own room at home. My grandparents let me paint it burnt orange, and I filled it with Asian inspired decor. Because of my mother's depression, I would sit for hours behind my closed door, writing and daydreaming. The feeling of freedom was foreign to me. It was intoxicating.

I filled journals with spiritual groanings and self-loathing—"Father" interjected every few sentences (as if He forgets who I'm writing to every few minutes) and "if it is your will" at the end of each entry—a daily, self-inflicted penance. I wrote Noah's name throughout. I wrote about the first high school party I went to and the sins I saw: kissing in cars and holding hands. Everything was laced with intensity.

I would sometimes sneak out and jump the fence into the open field across the street. I'd go for long walks with no specific destination, exploring for hours barefoot, electrified with a passion for living fully. It was rising in me, and it burned hot. Sometimes I would go outside in the middle of the night and dance to the music in my head, under the stars with my hands raised high.

When I was seventeen years old, I decided that I did not want to do my senior year. I had only two classes left to take, things at home were hard, and I wanted so desperately to marry Noah. The only reasons I was hesitant were that I would never have that classic senior photo of myself wearing a drape, like every girl has, and I wouldn't be able to sit in the top row of the bleachers for chapel, which was a huge deal in high school. But I quickly decided that going to college early would be so much better than having a photo and a place to sit, and I became determined to make it happen. Every day, I secretly applied to colleges as if I were a senior. I promised them I would take the two classes I needed during the summer at the local community college. One by one, the acceptance letters came, and I intercepted them at the mailbox before anyone else saw them. Soon I had four letters of acceptance hidden in my journal and several scholarships as well.

One morning I decided to show my mother what I was hiding in my room. She was speechless, and although she didn't say yes, she got out of my way. My skill with the violin ended up getting me a full scholarship to Erskine College in South Carolina, but when I went to the community college to sign up for the classes I needed, I was met with rooms full of high school dropouts and got nervous. I marched right home and called Erskine up on the phone to see if their full scholarship offer would still stand if I got my GED instead. Like my mom, they didn't say yes, but they didn't say no. Two weeks later I had a GED in hand and I was well on my way to college.

A few weeks after starting college, I went back to my high school campus to watch my sister play volleyball. I was so excited to return and see my old classmates, who still had another year to go. One of the first people I saw was my old PE coach, and I ran to give her a hug. Before I could embrace her, she kicked me out of the gym because my shorts were too short. She sent me walking down the side of the road like an unwanted child. And just like that, I was out of the family that I had grown to love. A family that had stepped in when mine was falling apart.

COLLEGE

I arrived at Erskine College with swollen chipmunk cheeks from having my wisdom teeth removed just days before. Mom helped me move my carefully chosen things into the bright, spacious dorm room in a beautiful, one-hundred-year-old house on the campus. As she left, she handed me a box of oatmeal. In the same moment, my roommate Kandi moved in with armfuls of snacks and drinks.

"Have all you want!" Kandi said sweetly.

She also showed me the most giant container of washing detergent I had ever seen. "It's to share!" she said with enthusiasm.

The campus of the small, Christian, liberal arts college was steeped in history. The buildings were built the century before, and giant trees towered over them.

That first evening, after I had hung my collage of Noah pictures and straightened my things, I ran into the hall and shouted, "I want to watch an R-rated movie!"

Someone heard me, and a group of Christian-school graduates invited me to their room to watch Orange County. I eyed the door for the shadow of my mother's feet, but they never appeared. That semester, while girls were getting drunk at parties, I was buying spaghetti strap tank tops and binge watching R-rated movies in my room.

Freshman orientation felt like camp. At seventeen, I should have been a senior in high school; instead, I sat in a room of eighteen-year-old freshmen, playing get-to-know-you games. In one game we were supposed to say what we were majoring in and why.

"Hi, I'm Megan, and I'm majoring in biology because I want to be a doctor."

"I'm John, and I am majoring in education because I want to teach high school math."

It went around the table until it got to me. "Hi, I'm Helen Joy, and I'm majoring in music performance, and I want to make people cry when I play my violin," I said in a dramatic, Scarlett O'Hara sort of way.

The whole room stared at me blankly, like I was an alien of some sort, then they all erupted with laughter.

After fall break I found out the hard way that "have all you want" did not mean that I should completely drain my roommate every week of forty dollars worth of food. After she brought it up to me in a note with a smiley face, I was embarrassed that I was so naive. I developed greasy skin and acne for the first time in my life and discovered, at the end of the first semester, that I had been leaving face cleanser on my face all day instead of lotion. I consider my first semester a detox.

The day after my final exam, I returned home to watch my mother walk down the aisle to marry a man I didn't like.

When my second semester began, I started finding my people. Rebekah was from my small town. She was untouchably beautiful and popular and made all the boys zone out when she was around. I had worked with her at my first job in high school, and I felt childish and clumsy next to her. She remembered me as the homeschooler who spent lunch copying quotes into a journal and saying, "I'm horny about going to this concert tonight," because no one had told me that it meant a different kind of excited. She drove me to and from Erskine sometimes, and every trip we made I fell more in love with her. Not only was she gorgeous, but she was adventurous and silly, and we laughed until our sides hurt.

Catherine was the classic all-American girl. She seemed perfect: tall, blond, and wholesomely beautiful. She had dozens of friends and was always smiling. Catherine had spotted me during orientation and heard me telling one of my wild stories from childhood. "That girl over there is lying," she whispered to someone. Months later, she realized that I was, in fact, telling the truth, and my crazy stories were not made up to get attention. Catherine turned out to be the very best kind of friend, the kind that never leaves, and she still laughs at my stories.

Katie was tall and stunning with dark hair that hung down her back. She had a beautiful voice and a beautiful heart. Melanie was my sporty friend. She was tall and athletic, an Army brat who wasn't used to having roots. She effortlessly joined our friendship circle, and we five became inseparable.

I had four tall friends with short me in the middle. Despite being the weird one, I felt a sense of belonging like I had never experienced before. My "too-muchness" was welcomed with open arms, like I was a missing puzzle piece that fit in just right.

For spring break Rebekah and I were invited to Melanie's grandmother's house in Florida for the week. Early the first day, I was sitting on a wooden bench wearing a thin skirt. I scooted over along the wood and got a hundred tiny, prickling splinters in my backside. That first day on the beach was windy. I fell asleep on my stomach, wrapped in a towel for warmth, but my legs were sticking out. When I woke up I had the worst sunburn imaginable on the backs of my legs. The next several evenings I spent lying over a couch while my new friends slathered me with vinegar and picked dozens of splinters out of my butt. I remember thinking that these girls would probably be lifelong friends. I was right.

The next day I started my period and bemoaned the fact that I couldn't wear a bathing suit to the beach.

"Why not?" they asked.

I explained to them that I had never been able to wear a tampon. They immediately loaded me into the car, and we went to Walmart to get some. They picked out small, smooth, teen ones—nothing like the super-plus cotton ones Mom had given me when I was thirteen. They stood outside the door, coaching me step by step until I had done it successfully. The key had been the last step, which I had missed for years: *Remove the applicator.*

The very last day of freshman year, I did my final load of laundry before leaving. I had felt for months that my clothes were never clean. Dirt stains would stick around through several washes, and I would often need to change several times throughout the day. While waiting for my clothes to dry I read, for the first time, the words on the side of the giant container of detergent my roommate had brought with her on our first day: **This is not a detergent.** I scanned the container and saw that it was, in fact, not a detergent, but a fabric softener. I laughed for an hour straight, packed up my room, and headed home.

My second year at Erskine was filled with pure fun. I don't think I did much schoolwork that year. My friend group grew, and I was always doing something purely for enjoyment. It felt foreign. Things back home were dark and poisonous. Sisters would call me, crying. Sometimes I wasn't even allowed to come home because I was viewed as an unwanted guest. I tried to push down the guilt of enjoying my life and not helping back home.

The freedom I felt at college brought new obsessions of getting Noah to marry me. I wouldn't turn eighteen till October, but the milestone burned in me. When I was eighteen, we could officially elope—if he would have me.

I didn't know it, but the previous spring, Noah had designed, and had a local artist fashion, a diamond ring for me. He asked my mother for my hand in marriage repeatedly for six months, the ring burning a hole in his pocket. But she violently opposed the proposal. The closeness built through the previous few years between her and Noah dissolved. My mama believed that women were under her parents until they were under their husbands, and even though I was grown up enough to be in college, I wasn't my own person; I was still hers.

One day in early September, during the first week of my sophomore year, Noah asked me anyway. He had a backpack of rose petals and spread them on the riverbank while I stood with my eyes closed. My "yes" wasn't even in question. When I returned to my mother's house to show her my ring, she went into her room and closed the door.

That year, I roomed with a quirky, introverted girl. Brandy was a year older than me and was adopted from Korea. She played violin too.

A friend snuck out the night I got engaged and hung up posters around campus announcing the surprise candlelight service, which is the way girls announced their engagements at Erskine. She was the only one who knew. I hid in our room, giggling and hiding under my covers, trying to hide my identity as the newly engaged. That night, all of the girls gathered in a circle outside our dorms, passing around a lit candle and singing:

Tell me why the ivy twines
Tell me why the stars do shine
Tell me why the sky's so blue
And I will tell you
Just why I love you

When the candle got to me, I puffed it out and fell on my knees, beaming through my tears. I was rushed with giddy friends and promptly thrown into the fountain in my overalls.

Brandy got to room with a distracted, lovesick, wedding-planning-crazy Helen Joy, but she tolerated me well. She cheered with me every morning when I changed the number of days until the wedding on the whiteboard outside our room. We consumed pickles at alarming rates and feasted on ramen noodles so we wouldn't have to go to the cafeteria. We watched TV curled up on the orange, silk couch that used to be my grandmother's.

That spring was filled with high teas and socials. It was also filled with extreme nausea and mood swings brought on by a birth control patch that my body tried to reject.

One week after my sophomore year ended, I would walk down the aisle. Despite the love story Noah and I wove throughout my teenage years, it turned out that the boy I loved would not be my rescuer. Not even close.

STOLEN

A few years after moving in with my grandparents, my mom started cleaning houses. Although she tried to provide for five girls with needs, escape from poverty seemed futile. She was worn out and ragged with nothing but scrubbing the pristine floors of the wealthy ahead of her. Then she was introduced to a man. He was a dentist who was in seminary, and my grandparents had met him and handpicked him for my mom. We helped her get ready for her first date with him, her first date since Dad left. We dressed her, made her up, and sent her out the door, waiting expectantly for her to return. We wanted her to be happy.

"It is a resounding no," she said when she returned from her date. His weak handshake put her off from the very first moment. "It was like touching a dead fish." We didn't expect a second date, but next thing we knew, he had bought her a new car, paid our school tuition, and sent her perfume from Paris. He was going to rescue her, and she was primed for it.

A week after they met, he and Mom drove me two hours to a hospital to get my wisdom teeth out. He acted like he was my dad, and I hated him for it. A week later, my first week of college, they got engaged.

"The person who kisses me has to marry me," Mom said coyly. And so he asked, and so they kissed.

The weekend after my first exams, when most people were crashing on their parents' couch and being fed copious amounts of homemade food, I was sobbing my way down the aisle at my mother's wedding. My sisters and I were dressed in long red gowns, and everyone sighed and tilted their heads thinking, *Look how happy they are to finally have a dad.* But we were crying because we were angry. Not one of us liked him, and more than that, we couldn't stand how our mother had transformed in his presence. I felt abandoned at that altar, tossed to the side for a man. I felt that at eighteen it shouldn't hurt that much, but the pain was sharp, and it gutted me. My sisters were sixteen, fourteen, ten, and six, and I wanted to gather them to me like a mother hen because it felt like we were orphans.

I returned to school, and a few weeks later Mom called to tell me she was pregnant. It was the ultimate betrayal. She was forty-two, and I was hours away at college. Several weeks later she called me in tears with the news that on the ultrasound that day two babies showed up. Twins. When I didn't think it could get any worse, she told me we would be welcoming two brothers in the fall, ruining our all-girl streak. I didn't want them, not one bit.

That fall, two days after my engagement, I waited by the phone in music theory class for the news that the twins had been born. I was the only person on campus waiting for news of new siblings. At last they were born, and I made the two-hour trip to visit them in the hospital. I felt like a stranger, like I should have brought flowers. My new ring sparkled, but my mom didn't say a word about it. I went to the state fair to ride roller-coasters and left the hurt in the hospital room.

As the years wore on, Mom seamlessly filled the gap between children and grandchildren with her two boys, James and John. My brothers came to my bedside when I had my first child, their four-year-old faces curious and scared. Mom handed down their tiny clothes and her breast pump to me. As they have grown alongside my own children, I have come to love every bit of their boyish charms. James is kind and gentle. He's always looking for better ways to do things, and he's smart. John is gregarious. He is a light in any room. He's wonderful at acting, and he's kind too.

The marriage of my mother to her new husband meant constantly walking on eggshells, screaming and yelling, and penance. Every time I came home from college, Mom was less and less herself. Laughter was banished, and my mom's open-door policy was closed. She feared him so greatly that she ignored the needs of her children in order to please him. I, her own daughter, was not allowed to come home from college at times, and girls were not allowed to talk at the table.

So many other people loved him, but he stole our mother from us and broke her into someone unrecognizable. Mom rarely stood up to him; instead, she took her rage and poured it out onto us. I got the least of it, being away at college, but my sisters lived in perpetual hell. If I were to heap my father's suicide attempt on top of itself one hundred times, it wouldn't hurt as much as watching my family waste away under this man's heavy hand.

Mom left him several times over the years but always returned. Police were sometimes called, but the event was always tucked away and forgotten. She started keeping her toiletries and herbs hidden away because she was paranoid he was trying to poison her. She went to the church, begging the elders for permission to leave him. They didn't grant it, so she returned to lie on the ground and let him step on her.

For her fiftieth birthday, my sisters and I took my mom on a three-night cruise. In two short days we saw her open up like a flower. It was glorious, but it hurt to see, like looking into the sun. On the drive home I told her I would never speak to her again unless she left him. Screw the church. God knew the truth, end of story. She finally found the strength, and she left. Bit by bit we got our mother back. Laughter slowly returned to our table, and her doors were once again flung open wide to welcome us all back in. But we had scars.

CLUTCHING
YELLOW TULIPS

"I'm getting married today!" I shouted as I literally fell down a staircase, waking my drowsy bridesmaids who were draped all over the couches in the living room. I did not get hurt. Nothing could quench my joy that day. Nothing. I shucked shrimp in my wedding veil, and when I remembered that I hadn't planned for bridesmaid bouquets, Mama picked daisies from the side of the road and bunched them together. My photographer told me that I was the happiest bride she had ever seen. She was right.

We married in May, surrounded by five hundred friends and family. I was still a teenager at just nineteen. Many people attending that day had beseeched me not to get married yet, saying I was too young. My mom, freshly in her second bad marriage, whispered in my ear right before we walked over to the chapel, "If you don't want to go through with it, it's okay."

Despite the resistance, I walked down the aisle to marry my Noah. I felt radiant, dressed in white lace and clutching a bunch of yellow tulips. I came to him raw, hurt so many times it felt like I didn't have skin. I needed balm. Noah received me with invisible walls encircling his heart, hiding a hurt that he wouldn't name or let me touch. Even though I was the happiest I had ever been, I ugly-cried the whole walk down the aisle. Throughout the ceremony I bounced up and down on the tips of my toes like a child waiting to ride the merry-go-round. It felt like a line was being drawn in the sand, separating my old life from my new. Light flooded me, and I basked in its glow. I had made it to the good part of my life. I was finally free.

We left for our honeymoon covered in birdseed, the box of unopened love letters I had written him since I was fourteen lying on the back seat. We were both virgins, and our honeymoon was spent unraveling a lifetime of shame that had sheltered our bodies. I had been told sex was bad, dirty, and sinful my whole life, yet after one afternoon in a chapel I was expected to blossom like a flower. Still, it was sweet to be together. We honeymooned twenty minutes from our hometown at a great old lodge overlooking our majestic Blue Ridge Mountains. We went to the spa and had a couples massage just like grown-ups. The champagne was left only for Noah but with a wink in my direction, since I was two years away from being legal drinking age. We explored gardens and went for hikes, and after a week we returned to our tiny, white-painted home, ready to start our normal life together.

I loved being a wife. I looked up recipes and cooked in my apron, welcoming my husband home like I had seen in the movies. I loved playing house. One day, a few weeks into my marriage, one of my single friends told me I should do a striptease for Noah since now that I was married it would be glorifying to God. She made me a CD of rap music and gave me lessons on hip rolls. I waited for him by the door in my nightie, feeling foolish and giggly. When he came in I sat him on the couch and pressed play. He smiled, and I knew it was because it was hilarious to see. I closed my eyes, pushing away the discomfort I was feeling. I grabbed the wooden fireplace mantle to show off more sexy moves, and mid-body-roll, the whole thing came crashing down on me. My fantasy crashed down with it, leaving me standing half naked in a pile of shattered glass from the crystal wedding presents that had been displayed on it. I was a teenage bride exposed for what she was—a child. After a few seconds of staring at each other, mouths gaping, we both started laughing, long, hard laughs. We still laugh about it.

Things were glorious for several weeks until one August day, as we were packing for a trip to Boston, when Noah said something that reached in and touched a raw part of me as if he'd poured salt into a fresh wound. It was a small comment—so small that I can't for the life of me recall what it was—but piercing. I clawed at him. I said words I'd never said before. I felt hot and unbridled. Minutes later, in the wake of the violent episode, I glanced at his face. His eyes were wide with terror. That was when my light started fading.

Noah had graduated from college several years before, but because I still had two more years until I got my bachelor's degree, that fall we left our tiny house in the mountains and moved back to my college town and into a small apartment with grass growing through the floor in the corners of the rooms. We became the hosts for countless parties with my college friends. People would pack in every weekend and many weeknights as well. Friends would leave their liquor in our freezer since they couldn't have it on campus. It was sometimes standing room only. I cooked elaborate dinners and made endless batches of chocolate chip cookies. It was fun. I also started drinking for the first time in my life. That was fun too.

We had a close relationship with our neighbors. Spencer was in seminary on campus and had married Aurora, who was fresh from Mexico, just six months after our wedding. Aurora and I would bake cookies and head to the dorms with a gallon of milk in one hand and a box of cookies in the other. We sold them door to door until we had enough quarters to take our husbands to the movies and get a burrito from Moe's. We would thrift shop for hours and resell our goods to pay our rent. We laughed from our bellies as she made tacos for the four of us.

In between classes, orchestra, and teaching violin lessons, I would lovingly prepare carefully planned meals for Noah. But he would come into the kitchen, which was dirty with dishes and food, glance at the meal on the table, and say, "I'm going to get a burger; I'm not eating that." He would drive to a nearby town to eat while I cried into my cold plate of food. Soon, he turned his back when I reached for him in bed, and he started making negative comments about my appearance. Tiny jabs at me from his ever-growing fortress of a body. By Christmas it was obvious that I was not in the good part of my life after all. My fantasies were systematically smashed and, as months slipped by, I sank into a heavy darkness. We didn't speak of my violent outburst, but I knew that it ate away at his love for me. There would be many more outbursts to come.

In the first semester of my junior year I was enrolled in a required class called Introduction to Art. We were assigned a self-portrait project. Noah and I had bought an expensive digital camera with our wedding money, and after years of using film, I could practice and see the results immediately. I ran home from class, filled my bathtub with mud, and crawled in, covering myself. I hit the timer over and over until I got the shot I wanted: me, wide eyed, reaching towards the lens. When presentation day came, I sat in the audience and watched baseball players drone on about their wrinkled poster boards of cut out baseballs and pictures of their girlfriends. When my turn came, I took my place in the center of the room and pulled out the picture of me covered in mud. "I feel like every day I am crawling through mud, I said."

Everyone stared at me, silent. Then I saw the tiniest hint of a smile start in the corners of the professor's mouth. She got me, but nobody else did.

I became more violent with Noah. I would beat my fists at him and scratch at him like a wounded animal. His words became more hurtful as he retreated into himself. He shot them like arrows. I drank more. He was scared of me. I went to him every morning like a shamed whore, weeping with guilt, but he would not take me back. He hardened, calloused, and shut me out.

One time we went to a concert with friends to see my favorite band, Nickel Creek. We were up in the top row with hardly anyone around, and they started playing the song I had dubbed our love song on my sixteenth birthday, "When You Come Back Down." Filled with nostalgia, I reached for Noah's hand and started softly singing along. Noah whispered viciously, "I didn't come here to hear you sing!"

The raw place inside of me was pierced again, and I jumped up and ran several rows down, where I found an empty seat. I started rocking and scratching at my skin in the dark, my pounding heart drowning out the music. When the concert was over and the standing ovation had ended, I kept my tear-stained face down and ran to our car without saying goodbye to our friends. Once we were in the car I didn't say a word, but I could feel the pain building and I didn't know how to make the pressure stop. Noah drove casually, acting like nothing had happened. At a stoplight I threw open the car door, grabbed the keys, and stood in front of the glaring headlights. "I want to die! I want to die!" I cried as I dug the keys into the milky white flesh of my forearms.

The summer after my junior year, we returned to North Carolina to work since there were no jobs in our small college town. Noah was trying to start a real estate career and I worked at Pier 1 and lifeguarded at the YMCA. The entire summer was full of unpredictable, violent episodes from me; I barely remember anything else except that our kitchen sink was always full. I don't recall the occasion, but one time Noah corrected me in the car while holding a bright pink cake in his lap. Enraged, I stuck my hands in it and started smearing it all over the car and myself, screaming hateful things. He dropped me by the side of the road, and I was forced to walk to his dad's house a few miles away covered in pink icing.

Noah would come home from work hours late without calling. He shrugged when I cried about it. I would usually chug liquor and threaten suicide. One stormy evening it got so bad that I took all my clothes off and ran into the street with a knife. I stood in the rain, crying out for help, wanting to stab myself. I lay down on the warm pavement, waiting for Noah to come for me. But I knew he wouldn't come, he wouldn't rescue me. I knew it deep down. When I finally pulled myself off the asphalt, shrouded in shame, I went inside to find him on the couch, watching a movie like nothing had happened.

We returned to South Carolina for my senior year and to our old apartment, which was filled with memories of shattered dreams. I had lost nearly all of my self-worth. I would get sips of it from other people—when I played violin, when I was fun at a party, when people admired my photography. But it was all a veneer.

That year, instead of crawling through mud in my bathtub, I became brilliant and manic. I would wake up in the night with ideas that I would jot down. My days and nights were consumed with pictures that I saw in my head and had to create. I taped black trash bags to my windows and invited groups of girls from school over to shoot nude portraits of them. They were tasteful and artistic, draped and shadowed. I got high from it. I came up with a brilliant concept for an installation for the college's spring art show. I could barely speak about it, the ideas were flying so fast. In the end, I framed thirty black and white self-portraits and connected them with red ribbon to a candle in the middle. "I Am Woman," it was titled. I was Eve. I was an African woman. A mother. Someone from the Renaissance. A girl getting her first period. I spent hours away from friends creating these snapshots of womanhood, hunched over my camera, desperate to paint what I was seeing in my head. I abandoned housework, cooking, all the wifely duties I had taken pride in the year before.

Despite my obsessions, I miraculously graduated from college, fulfilling a promise to my mother, and Noah and I went back to North Carolina for good. We moved into an apartment with a screened porch. It was fresh and empty, but it soon filled up with the same dangerous tunes, a tango of wishing to die and trying to tame the sparks of excessive creative thinking in my brain. My skin felt electric. I would go onto the porch naked, pull the shades down so that no one could see anything but my legs, and paint for hours, temporarily soothed. Once when I was painting on the porch, I accidentally locked myself out of the house. After waiting for an hour, I cut a hole in the screen, draped my body in a wet, freshly painted oil canvas, and knocked on the neighbor's door and asked to use their phone to call my husband to come home and let me in. I have that canvas hanging in my kitchen today.

Noah and I fought for hours at a time. It was a cycle that was sucking us under the waves. The deeper I went under, the more I lashed out. The more he went under, the more he shut down. I reached; he retreated. I would wake up in the mornings with curse words carved all over my skin with a pen and blood; memories of the night before felt like a dream.

I was freaking out. I filled books with lists of ways I could be better. I spent hours making lists and still could not manage to get anything done. We had been going to marriage counseling since before we got married. One day I was babbling on about lists regarding laundry organization, and our counselor set her clipboard to the side and said, "Helen Joy, I think maybe you have bipolar disorder." She referred me to a psychiatrist who told me I most certainly did. The diagnosis hung in the air, and I observed myself from afar, thinking, *Maybe life doesn't have to be this hard.*

I had been taking the mood stabilizer for only a few days when I found myself leaning against the kitchen sink, doing the dishes. Noah came up behind me and said something critical, another arrow from his fortress of a heart. It was something that just a week before would have sent me down a path of rage and mutilation. But this time I felt something different. Space.

SECRETS

I have this vivid memory of myself. I was ten, curled up under my bed on the hardwood floor, waiting for someone to find me. My cousin was over to play, and I believed she belonged to me alone. She was very special to me, just my age, and I didn't want to share her with my sisters. That day she chose to play with them instead of me, probably because I was being bossy. Even as I type this, I feel humiliation rising in my body; it's silly, it's childlike, it's normal. No great trauma happened. My cousin just didn't want to play with me and I should get over it. I went to my mother in the kitchen, tears on my freckled cheeks, and told her what had happened. She was cooking or talking on the phone, and she told me to stop and dismissed me to the other room, just like I have done to my own children many times. I lay on my stomach under my bed, and I could feel a pit inside me, hard, burning, decaying. I waited for hours, but no one came searching for me.

The first time I tried to kill myself, I was twelve. I wore a skirt that didn't touch my knees and as punishment was told I would be staying home with my five-year-old sister, Georgia Ann, instead of going to the movies with the family. As everyone piled into the van, I cried so hard I could barely breathe. My wailing scared Georgia Ann, and even though I wanted to comfort her and hold her to my chest, I could not stop.

I rushed to my room, grabbed my Lisa Frank journal, and violently scratched out a suicide note. Three pages covered in "I want to die" and one filled with both a desperate desire to end my life and regret about hurting my family. I had no control over whatever was driving me; I felt as if someone else inhabited my body. I left the journal open on my mom's pillow, grabbed the belt to her robe, and went to the stairs, where I tried to hang myself over and over and over from the thin, white stair railing that was just within my reach. I would pick up my feet and hang by my neck until I couldn't stand it. I didn't know what I was doing. I finally gave up and slumped to the floor in a pile. I was so confused and so ashamed. The baby was crying and looking at me for comfort.

When Mom came home that evening, I strangely wanted her to know, but I was scared to tell her. Instead, I left my journal on her bed, open to the suicide note, and hid in the bushes outside to watch through the window. My chest was thumping. She came in, glanced at it, closed it, and set it on the side table without ever saying a word to me. I didn't tell another soul for twenty years.

The second time I tried to kill myself, I was a heartbroken and manic young bride, married just shy of two years. It was the night of my senior sorority dance, and I felt radiant, dressed in a long, flowing, blue silk dress. Despite my exterior, I was filled with cheap liquor and death.

On that beautiful spring evening, when Noah and I arrived at the country club in Anderson, South Carolina, my skin was alive with the warm breeze, and the smell of blooming flowers filled the night air. There was drinking and dancing outside under a white pavilion. The whole scene evoked the nostalgic gaiety of a different era. All my senses were heightened, and I was with all my best friends just weeks before graduation. The energy I felt inside was so great I thought I might just pop. After drinking more, I got on the dance floor and swayed across the floor, feeling like I was the most beautiful woman there, feeling eyes on me from all directions. People loved me. Nothing had changed since I was a toddler. But every time I glanced at Noah, hoping he would notice me in all my joy, he looked ashamed and turned his back—just like he did when I was a cheerleader. I wanted him to join me, to swing me around him like I was made of air. I begged him to dance, but he shrugged me off, whispering, "You're embarrassing me."

Frantic with hurt, I ran to the parking lot and paced back and forth, my mind searching for ways to suppress the feelings of rejection that overwhelmed me. I rummaged through our car to see if I could find anything sharp to dull my pain. I saw a half-full bottle of ibuprofen tablets and, without thinking, gulped them all down.

I felt like I was in a perfume ad. Glancing back at the party, I darted into the darkness onto the club's golf course. My bare toes touched the cool grass, and short bursts of my breath pierced the night as the music grew faint behind me. I finally stopped running and fell into a heap of blue silk. I lay on my back on the damp grass, overcome with the vastness of the galaxies Dad always talked about. I felt so small, so inadequate.

My body shook as I watched the stars and blinked hot tears down my cheeks. Time slowed my heart to a quiet beat. *This is the end,* I thought. I wondered if my husband would even cry for my cold body on this dew-soaked mound.

It felt like hours before I realized that death never came. I wasn't relieved. I was ashamed. No one was looking for me. The pit inside of me burned with loneliness and weighed my body down, just like it did in that little girl under the bed.

Walking back to the party, my dress wet and stained with grass, I was worried that people had been anxiously looking for me and even more terrified that they hadn't. I walked up to the veranda and glanced around at the joyful gathering. I had not even been missed.

This, too, was a secret I kept for years.

Secrets. They kill you.

SISTERS

When I look back on my life and see a vast desert of hard things, I also see that God has rained manna down on me in the form of my sisters.

We grew up little stairsteps of blond girls. Bows on all of their heads, all taught to act the same way. We each were given two names (Julianna's sounded like two) and went by them. When Mama called for us, it sounded like she was calling ten children: Helen Joy, Katie Beth, Julianna, Georgia Ann, Sarah Grace. We looked the same, but below the surface each one of us was complex and magnificently unique. Mama would always remind us, "Remember, your sisters will be your very best friends." And we were.

Katie Beth came into the world two years and one day after my birth. We missed sharing a birthday by mere hours because Mom managed to keep it together during my second birthday party at Chuck E. Cheese and delivered Katie Beth early the following morning. Growing up, the two of us shared birthday parties, and I did not like it one bit. I could barely bask in the glory of being adored before everyone had moved on to adoring Katie Beth the next day, and she didn't even like the attention. She was opposite of me—gentle, quiet, and shy.

Despite my initially feeling jealous of her, Katie Beth has always been one of my very best friends. She has the most tender soul of anyone I know. She is always serving and sacrificing. She wanted to be a nurse and a mom when she grew up, which fit her nature perfectly. She always had her hands full of bugs and lizards to study and protect. Her long hair, which curled on the ends, her darling lisp, and her mischievous smile made everyone fall in love with her.

When Dad shot himself, I watched Katie Beth's heart begin to close. She was a young bride when, ten days after I had my first baby, she miscarried hers. His name was Gideon. The calluses grew. A year later, she got pregnant at the same time her husband started a public affair. She was stripped bare and staying alive for her baby took every ounce of her strength. After walking the streets of San Diego in the wee morning hours, the sisters convinced her to come back to North Carolina.

At six months pregnant, my sister moved in with Noah and me. I was seven months along with my second child, and we would spend our nights sitting on the couch, watching mysteries and eating ice cream while our bellies grew. After I went to sleep, she stayed up for hours in agony, and her eyes were swollen every morning. We had just moved to a new neighborhood, and the neighbors called us sister wives, curious as to why a man and two very pregnant women would live together.

When I gave birth to my son Sullivan, Katie Beth was in the room, the only family member to see one of my babies born. She stayed pregnant long after she was supposed to. After her due date came and went, her husband flew back for the birth and sat, indifferent, empty of remorse, in our living room. My sister cried on the floor, begging him to love her. Without blinking, all he said was, "No." Her heart closed up, only to have it opened back up weeks later when her daughter finally came into the world.

Today, Katie Beth is not a nurse. She's a cop, determined to serve people through justice. She is still compassionate and pure, but you have to work your way through the callouses to get to the tenderness. She's worth it, and to be loved by her is one of life's greatest gifts. Katie Beth always says "we" when she talks to me. Lumping me in with her as she talks about anything and everything. "What are we gonna do?" "What should we make for dinner?" I know she will protect me, defend me, care for me, just like she did for her precious lizards. We are indeed a we.

When I was three, I was taken to the hospital where I got to hold beautiful, newly born Julianna—the only one of us with a pretend double name. We called her Poker Face. She never smiled unless she wanted to, and no amount of tickling and cooing would make her do it. Julianna was a pensive child, a serious child with a brilliant mind. She was always the princess in our plays, and she ruled with grace and justice. She had wide eyes that were full of depth and full, cherry-red lips. Julianna always liked breaking the mold of what was expected. She stuck by her desires and wasn't swayed by what other people were doing. I remember her around the age of six, dressed to the nines in a cheetah-print leotard under a see-through red negligée we played dress up in. She was wearing lipstick, carrying a purse, and wearing glorious high heels, posed on the hood of our car, and we were all giggling at her. She didn't bat an eye. I watched in awe as this tiny sister of mine marched to the beat of her own drum, and it stirred a deep desire in me to be like her.

Julianna has grown to be the most incredible woman. She mothers her three girls with such attentiveness and still finds time to feed her mind with the knowledge that she craves. When most moms are taking a nap or watching TV while their babies are sleeping, she is often devouring thick books on philosophy. She's complex. She wears heels and kicks ass as a tax practitioner, and sometimes she protects her family by fending off rogue squirrels who try to invade her home. There is no one like her, and I'm glad she's mine.

Georgia Ann was born when I was seven, and she was the greatest gift any girl my age could want. She was a real, live baby doll. I spent the days caring for her, sleeping with her, protecting her. She was a cherub with bouncy blonde curls, big, blue eyes, and cheeks so chubby you wanted to pinch them. She was the flower girl in a dozen weddings, often recycling a dress from the previous one. Georgia was uncomplicated and easy to please. Kind to animals and a lover of the outdoors. She was also hilarious and kept us entertained with songs and skits. She surprised us all with a rough patch during her sixth-grade year at the Christian school we attended. She carved a cuss word into her desk and blew up a classmate's Barbie doll in the microwave. Her pain from Dad's suicide attempt and Mom's remarriage had to escape somewhere.

Georgia Ann lived with Noah and me off and on when we were newlyweds and when I was new mama. She stayed with us on school nights, and I packed her lunches. On game nights, we lectured her about boys and safety. She is equally sister and daughter to me. Today, she teaches Spanish to middle schoolers and endears herself to students with that same quirky humor that makes us all laugh till we cry. I still feel like a proud mama to her.

I found out about Sarah Grace when I was eleven years old, after my mother and father sat the four of us girls on the bed, lined up oldest to youngest. With tear-filled eyes, Mom said, "First we had Helen Joy, and we liked her so much we decided to have another baby, so we had Katie Beth. And soon we had another baby, Julianna, and she needed a sister, so we had Georgia Ann."

We stared at them and looked to the empty spot on the bed next to Georgia Ann. Our parents' faces were filled with fear and uncertainty. This was not planned. This was an accident. I fell on the floor, sobbing, and covered my face.

I had no clue how we could take care of another baby, but she came nevertheless, another girl. My sisters and I were given the job of naming her. Sarah Grace was born into trauma. She never knew our father. She never knew a family unit, but she did have five mamas and plenty of arms to hold and soothe her. Sarah Grace carries with her resilience and has weathered two broken homes. She is a prolific artist who finds loveliness in the rubbish. As a ten-year-old she used to take scissors to thrift store clothes to reinvent them into something she could wear. When she entered public high school, after being homeschooled nearly her whole life, she wore her funky creations proudly and didn't back down when her peers pointed and whispered. She ended up making a difference in that school. She created a real wave of change, which ironically culminated in her being crowned homecoming queen one beautiful fall night. By the time she graduated, everyone else was wearing funky things too.

People often ask me if I am closer to one sister over the others, and I always tell them, "It depends on the day. It depends on the season." Since each is unique, I feel like I have a wide range of support around me. Katie Beth comes and watches my kids when I am overwhelmed; she mows my high grass and plants flowers for me in the winter. Julianna talks to me for hours, patiently, not judging. She praises genuinely, in ways that touch corners of my heart. Georgia Ann is compassionate and loves deeply through lovingly made meals. Sarah Grace uplifts everyone around her and brings joie de vivre.

Mama was right. They are my very best friends—built into the infrastructure, the roots of my life, and steeped with history that often can't even be spoken. More than anything, every single one of my sisters knows. They just know. They are manna from heaven, I tell you.

BECOMING MAMA

Before I ever had babies in my belly, I had mothered four children in my heart.

I only ever wanted to be a mama. I never dreamed of a handsome prince, but I always dreamed of babies. When I was twelve I frequently said I would never marry and would instead move to China and adopt 101 Chinese babies. (This was based on a movie I had seen called *Inn of the Sixth Happiness.* My email address all through high school was chinesebabies101@yahoo.com. Don't email me, though, I've forgotten the password.) In high school, when the other girls were pinning up magazine clippings and photos of boys they liked, I was tucking away baby clothes in my hope chest.

When I got engaged, I went to an obstetrician who didn't even examine me since I was a virgin. He prescribed a patch for birth control. Every time I put it on, I prayed it would fail. I imagined myself walking across the stage at college graduation ripe and pregnant, but to my dismay the patch worked just like it should have.

When I was diagnosed with bipolar disorder, I took it in stride and rejoiced that I felt better when medicated. A few short months after feeling normal, I let out a long sigh of relief—I could have a baby now; I wouldn't be crazy. At my next appointment I told them I was ready to have a baby and asked if I could get pregnant, considering the medicine I was taking. A doctor, whose face I have chosen to erase, told me, "Bipolar people shouldn't have children."

"Watch me," I said as I left, never to return again. That day began a long decade of living unmedicated.

I removed all medication from my body and got pregnant the first try, which would later prove to be a miracle. I had previously taken dozens of pregnancy tests. Even with our low income, I would buy them every time I thought a happy accident might have occurred. Once, when I was buying a pregnancy test from the local CVS, the redneck clerk with missing teeth said, "Hope you is, or hope you ain't?" I asked her to repeat herself, since I didn't understand. "Hope you is, or hope you *ain't?*"

"Oh. Hope I is!" And did I ever.

On the morning of our third wedding anniversary, I got out of bed at the crack of dawn to pee on the stick. I wasn't hopeful. Before the time was up, I glanced over and saw a positive sign flash on the screen, and I lost my freaking mind. I ran screaming into the room and woke Noah up by swinging the test in front of his face. "Get that out of my face! Ugh! You peed on that," he grumbled. It took him all nine months to warm up to the idea, but he emerged a champion father. In all my pregnancies, he never once was excited about a positive test before his morning coffee, but even if I had a hundred pregnancies, I still don't think I could wait to tell him.

Good thing I wanted a baby so desperately, because the next nine months were so brutal I felt like jumping off a cliff. I had what is called hyperemesis gravidarum, which is basically puking every few minutes almost every day of the entire pregnancy, right up to delivery. It was horrible and lonely, and it was the first time I experienced what it feels like to have people get tired of you after a month of caring about it.

I was so sick I couldn't even drive without puking, so I would carry an extra-large cup from the gas station to throw up in at stoplights. I discovered that a produce bag in the grocery store was super heavy duty, so I bought a lot of produce and used the bags in public. I can still see the horrified face of a white-haired woman as I threw up in the bag while shopping, tied a knot, tossed it in my purse, and walked away. I had to be hospitalized for dehydration and put on drugs that didn't work. Still, I was the happiest person on earth because I was going to be a mama.

I found out I was having a boy at the doctor's office (this was before gender reveals were a thing). I held it together till we left, then cried big, hot, heavy tears. I didn't know how I would love a boy; I had only mothered girls. And more importantly, how would he love me? That day, my mother-in-law took me to buy a rocking chair upholstered in blue ticking, and I bought a tiny pair of little-boy shoes. From that point on I felt much better and delved into the world of boys with such enthusiasm I couldn't contain my joy. We named him Barclay after a far-removed cousin on Noah's side. I told people the name and got scathing responses, but I didn't care. As I awaited his arrival with my head hung over the toilet, I could see myself holding him, and it was romantic and radiant like a sunset.

Barclay was born during an ice storm in February 2009. I was nearly two weeks overdue and exhausted, yet I was elated that I was finally going to hold my first baby in my arms. Shaking, I brought him forth with one last push, fifty hours after labor began. I cried the ugliest, most beautiful cry when they placed him on my chest, and Noah finally got it. He got the love I have been carrying around for nine months. I put Barclay to my breast before the lactation consultant could even get to my room. In shock, she asked, "How did you even know what to do?" Quietly, without looking at her, I said, "Well, because I watched my mama do it."

After a day of constant care in the hospital, the nurses loaded all three of us in our truck, *and they let us take him home.* We were in shock. How did they know we could keep that tiny, seven-pound thing alive? When we got home, Noah assembled the cradle. I had waited my whole life for this baby, went past my due date, and still had not put the cradle together. That just goes to show how sick I was. While Noah worked, I held Barclay's little body close to me, my own body aching from birth, as he screamed. I thought, "Where is this kid's mother?"

It didn't even take a day for me to quickly and naturally fall into mothering. I wasn't surprised at how much I loved him, because I had a lifetime of love waiting for him. I was, however, surprised at how lack of sleep affected me so much. It was hard to make it through midnight nursing sessions, dragging myself out of bed, over to the crib, and to the rocking chair. Everyone was telling me I could *not* put the baby in the bed with me, and their stories scared me to death. After six months, I had had enough and tucked that little boy in next to my warm body, and we both slept soundly for the first time. For the next baby, I didn't listen to anyone else, and by baby number three, mothering was a glorious celebration of my intuition.

But it wasn't all a fairytale. Barclay wasn't like my sister-babies; he cried every waking hour—and he had a lot of waking hours. We finally learned at nine months that an allergy to eggs and gluten were causing his extreme agitation. Nine years later, he would be diagnosed with ADHD, a partial explanation for his complex and difficult childhood. Those days and nights robbed me of the vision I had of myself as a mother, the redemptive mother I wanted to be. The whispers of self-doubt about my mothering would build to a scream over the years.

My next pregnancy was twins, and at eight weeks they became two little sacks without heartbeats. We waited weeks before a doctor would remove them, lifeless, in a surgery center off the side of a highway. If it's possible, I wanted that pregnancy more than any other, but that sorrow taught me a lot about grief and how to love people through it. Many people made vague offers of help or sent well wishes, but others actually showed up. That's when I felt loved; that's when I felt carried along in my mourning. I was so lonely, and I needed someone to sit with me in my grief, not someone to say the "right" thing in a hollow attempt to make it better. This period was the first time I was raw and open publicly, through my blog. I was met with a lot of support. I was met with hurting people. I wasn't alone, and that was transformative.

Four weeks after the twins were taken away, I tested positive with another baby. This time I was hesitant and wouldn't use the words, "We are having a baby," because I knew that wasn't a given anymore. When I saw that flicker of a beating heart at ten weeks, I exhaled a wave of love and expectancy that had built up. It was nearly a year of throwing up again and developing more love than I could hold as this new son grew on the inside, and Barclay grew on the outside. We named him

Sullivan after Sullivan's Island, which held such wonderful memories for me.

Sullivan was born on Valentine's Day, 2011, limp and gray following thirty hours of unmedicated labor and about thirty minutes of panic and chaos. After his head emerged, his shoulders got stuck and his body would not come out. Seeing his struggle and seeing the umbilical cord wrapped several times around his neck, the midwife pushed an emergency button and the room immediately filled with doctors and nurses. Noah quickly lifted me off of the birthing stool and threw me onto the bed across the room. A nurse sat on my belly, pressing down with all her might, and cried, "If you don't push, your baby is going to die!" Thank God my midwife was bold and maneuvered him out with her hands three minutes later instead of rushing me to a C-section that would most likely have ended in his death.

After he was taken to the warming table to be resuscitated, I lay there, limp. My body was broken, I was sure of it. I looked up at the white light above me and thought I must be dead. I just knew Sullivan was lifeless, too, because the room was eerily quiet, even though it was still filled with nurses and doctors who were trying to revive him. Everything was in slow motion. I didn't have the strength physically or emotionally to turn my face to try to see him. Suddenly, he breathed. He breathed! He cried the most beautiful, piercing cry. After he was x-rayed for broken bones and checked thoroughly, at last they placed him on me—and I felt afraid. Even though he was a big baby, he seemed so fragile. I didn't want to hurt him. But by the wee morning hours he was nestled against me, and I felt safe that he would stay.

As Sullivan was snuggling in as a newborn, Barclay was still struggling. Our bond was present, but it was jagged. I never felt that I could meet his needs or that the love I poured on him was accepted. Sullivan helped me see myself as a good mama for the first time. I did what my mama's intuition told me to do, and he responded. The closeness between us was staggering. He rarely cried, and I referred to him as my balm.

Six weeks after Sullivan was born, I experienced a life-changing event. With my precious newborn babe wrapped to me, I watched as his cousin breathed her first breath. My jaw dropped open as I locked eyes with her when her head appeared. It was my first time witnessing a birth rather than experiencing one. I supported my sister Katie Beth during her entire labor and, since my own birth was fresh in my mind, I knew exactly what to do. Because of this experience, I later became a birth doula, and I'm quite sure that was what I was created to be. Days after the birth of my niece, Rainy, my sister's breasts were engorged with milk, and her tiny girl, unable to latch on, was screaming to be fed. I put Sullivan to Katie Beth's breast, and he emptied her better than any breast pump could. I put Rainy to mine, and she filled up instantly, happily slipping into a milk coma in my arms. It was a magical, wonderful beginning to the mothering of "twin cousins."

After Sullivan, I sold all our baby stuff and all my pregnancy clothes, thinking I couldn't do it again. I couldn't love and have it taken away the way the twins were, the way Sullivan almost was. That didn't last but a year, then my perpetual hope returned like yellow tulips every spring. I wanted one more baby. I got pregnant pretty quickly and held to an unabashed hope that this baby would join our arms. I was wrong.

I miscarried. Then came another, and another. No matter what I did, no matter how badly I wanted these babies, I had miscarriages. Five babies gone, even though I loved them from the first moment I knew they existed. I experienced the lack of support that results when people have had enough of your sorrow. After three miscarriages in a row, no one shows up the for the third one.

For our last baby, we went to a fertility clinic to try and avoid another gut wrenching miscarriage. After some drugs and shots in my butt to help me ovulate, our Lucy Miller was conceived. It was a group effort, including me knocking on my sister's door at three in the morning for her to give me the shot before I attended a birth as a doula because Noah was too queasy about needles. But the medication was the golden ticket. This was the baby that would see it through to full term.

By the time our daughter was born, I had been working as a trained birth doula for years. Having a doula myself was important for this birth, and we found three women who would be on call for us. I did everything right to ensure that this baby wouldn't get stuck and that I could enjoy the birth I knew was possible. Still, Sullivan's traumatic birth echoed in my head, and I was nervous. I was still sick every day right up to when my labor began, and this labor lasted more than two weeks. I was in prodromal labor, having strong contractions without cervical change, and it did not let up. The experience stretched me as a person and as a mother in ways I couldn't have imagined.

The day after the baby was due, things finally started changing. My doula, my midwife, and my husband surrounded me as I labored. It was earth-shatteringly painful, and it was earth-shatteringly sacred. When she finally decided to descend, she got stuck in my birth canal. Nothing

I did helped, and with Sullivan's birth in the back of our minds, and through the strong urging of the doctor on call, we chose to bring her into the world via C-section.

As they were wheeling me back for surgery, they asked me, for charting purposes, why I was going into surgery, and I said, "I'm getting a boob job."

She was born pink and tiny and breathing.

Lucy's life was the first time I felt like God knew me, like He could see my desires and I wasn't just a number floating through the galaxies. God gave me a daughter. Pure and simple. Maybe He loved me after all.

We named her Lucy for my infamous great-aunt Lucy and Miller after our paternal grandmothers' maiden names, both which were Miller. All three of these women were beautiful creations who lived outside of the box.

Nurturing Lucy Miller was like dancing the most beautiful waltz. Every care for what others thought, or how I thought I should be, melted away, and it was pure. It was holy to love her and to be her mama.

NIGHTGOWN MAMA

She's swaying barefoot in the kitchen, cooking breakfast and humming quietly. Vivaldi is swelling from the stereo, filling the room with magic. She's feminine: floor-length, floral nightgown, soft and airy. Her long brown hair falls down her back in a thick braid, and her cheeks are flushed the color of the camellias outside our door. That's the picture I have of my mama. The house was always as it should be—formal and clean, filled to every corner with delicious smells from the kitchen.

All my life, I've wanted nothing more than to be a nightgown mama. Someone soothing and gentle. Someone lovely to look at and to inhale. In my imagination I can see her still, and I can see myself, flushed and feminine, nurturing and serving. I can see every detail of the dainty, sweeping nightgown I am dressed in. My children's faces light up in adoration when they look at me, and I can finally exhale.

How do I really look? I am half-naked with one fuzzy, lime-green sock on. My hair is stuck to the side of my face because it hasn't been washed in two days. I'm sweaty and mangled. I stumble down the stairs at the last minute and frantically start pouring cereal. No one can eat at the table, because it's covered with used paint brushes and portraits of dinosaurs. Chaos swells. I always forget appointments, I always forget to switch the laundry, I always forget where I put my keys. I'm a mess and always ashamed of it.

It hurts, this longing that I can't fulfill. I'm desperately sad that the days tick by and my children grow and I cannot bring myself into existence. Occasionally, the curtain is pulled back, and I will have glimpses of the good mom I am. Not the soft, feminine, nightgown mama, but the strong, creative mama with wells of love so deep you can't see the bottom. I can see the tired, crinkled eyes full of love. She views forts and art projects as things of beauty in her home and not a mess, claiming victory by placing a bunch of yellow tulips amongst the Legos and breadcrumbs. I can see the tenderness as she listens to a story told with excited eyes and adorable lisps. She is soft and warm. I can see the joy she brings to the home, the way she gathers them all together in a nest made of pure love. She is lovely, and there's no doubt that she loves hard. She dances in the moonlight, shrieking with joy. She's wild and gentle, and her heart is pure. And sometimes she wears a nightgown.

Dad surfing, Charleston, SC circa 1968

Mom, Helen Joy, Katie Beth
living in a trailer on a job site, Colorado, 1987

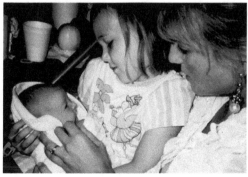

Mom, Helen Joy (big sister), Julianna,
Charleston, SC Mar 21, 1989

Helen Joy, Georgia Ann, Katie Beth, Julianna, flying
to the Canary Islands, Madrid, Spain, 1992

Mom and girls camping, Tenerife, Canary Islands 1992

Dad, Helen Joy, Julianna, Katie Beth, serving parents a
romantic dinner, Charleston, SC, circa 1996

Mom and girls, Easter, Charleston, SC, circa 1996

Helen Joy daydreaming in the yard, Charleston,
SC circa 1997

Helen Joy, wedding day
Hendersonville, NC, May 21, 2005

Sisters, Hendersonville, NC 2019

Family portrait, Hendersonville, NC 2018

PART

2

THE WIND

"I'm going to be the wind," I said to my best friend, Summer, over the phone. We were getting ready to go out to a Halloween concert that our friends performed each year, where covers like "Thriller" and "Bust a Move" would fill the chilly air of the indoor/outdoor brewery. It was the fall of 2016, and I had just turned thirty-one.

I had a long, blue dress that was perfect for billowing in the wind—I had worn it for maternity pictures two years before. It would flow behind me when I walked and make everything appear as if I were in a slow-motion music video. No one else would dress as the wind, I was sure of that. I felt so clever to have thought of it. To complement my dress I decided to spray my hair straight back so that it looked like the wind was blowing it. I emptied a whole can of hairspray in my hair as I arched my back over the edge of my unmade bed. Summer giggled at me while my mind raced and thoughts came faster than I could hold onto. I pictured it in my mind, the heads that would turn as I walked into the concrete courtyard of the brewery in my ethereal getup, the lustful eyes that would stare at me.

But no matter how much I sprayed it, my hair, long and heavy, would simply not stand off my back. Instead of feeling carefree, it felt like gooey noodles, lifeless and grotesque, sticking to my back. I stood looking in the mirror at my shattered dream when I realized Noah was ready to leave. I threw on a baggy dress, braided my hair in two braids, and stuck a coat hanger through them. Pippi Longstocking was my go-to costume. As much as I loved Pippi, it was far less enchanting than being the wind, so I became Pippi with a flask in her pocket, Pipi with an ache in her heart. On the way to the brewery we picked up another friend, who drew five dark freckles on my already freckled nose. I looked like a homeless clown. That now familiar ache was pulsing through me, and I wiped my tears away quickly as we drove to the concert. Once there, I felt painfully disconnected from everyone around me. It was like everything was taking place behind a pane of dirty glass. I observed everyone behind it moving and talking and having fun, and I felt separated. I felt alone. I drank too much and found myself leaning over the sink in the bathroom, looking into the mirror and searching for myself through my clouded eyes. Everything was a blur, and I couldn't find me no matter how long I stared. The emptiness I saw instead was deep and frightening. I felt the hate and annoyance of every person there heaped on me, and I knew I deserved it. No one would have hated the wind.

After the concert, we would usually go downtown for greasy bar food and post-dancing chatter. But this time I couldn't bring myself to go. I longed for my bed and the quiet of my home. I couldn't wait to get away from the consuming pain I was feeling being around people, and I asked to be taken home. Noah dropped me at our back door and sped off to join the fun.

As soon as I got inside, I paid the babysitter with a hurriedly scrawled check and waited until her car pulled into the dark street to let out a whimper. I sank to my knees and felt an electric pulsing in my body. I had been hanging on all night just to come home and fall apart. I clawed at the walls of my brain for some escape from the suffocating I felt, as if my mind were drowning in blackness.

I walked to the kitchen and, without thinking, pulled out the sharpest knife we had. The counter was cool against my belly as I held the knife to my wrist, pressing gently, watching my skin turn white around the blade. Before it broke the skin, I yanked it away and threw it into the drawer. Terrified, I ran up the long staircase to my room and fell into bed, jumping up seconds later as the drowning feeling intensified. I looked through Noah's sock drawer for the bottle of pain pills he had from a surgery months before. There were just three small pills left. I found another bottle prescribed to me after Lucy's birth, with half a pill. I laid them out in rows alongside all the ibuprofen I had. I looked up how many it would take to kill me, but before I knew if I had enough, I panicked and put them all back. I was breathless with panic. It felt like I wasn't in control of what I was doing.

I ran back to my bed, pulling the quilt over my head in a futile effort to hide from my own mind, from the thought that I was drowning. I threw off the covers, flew down the stairs to the liquor cabinet, and picked up a heavy bottle of tasteless vodka, sloshing it against my thigh as I went back up to the bedroom. I fell into bed with the bottle, intending to drink every drop with the hope that I would never wake up. But I couldn't bring myself to drink it. My father and his botched suicide attempt haunted me and the fear of death permeated my body. I ran back down with and shoved the bottle back into its empty spot on the shelf. I was delirious, grasping for anything to keep the darkness from swallowing me. When I closed my eyes, I saw the people from the brewery laughing at me, pointing at me, turning their backs on me. I needed to be numb, if only for a few seconds, so I could find my way back. My father's empty eyes seemed to stare at me through the darkness. I didn't want to end up like him.

I danced with death that night: touching, tempting, holding, inhaling, fantasizing with the things that could kill me. I was detaching from myself. I didn't die, but when the drowning subsided, I was left feeling cowardly and worthless. No one knew, and I was sure they would be disgusted if they did.

THE MERMAID

That Halloween night came and went, then faded into my memory. A week later, I was planning to go to a local fundraiser for children in the community. I had been looking forward to dressing up for it all year, and most of our friends were going to attend. Months before the event, I discovered a glittery, gold gown at a local thrift store for five dollars. From the foundation of the dress I built an elaborate fantasy of me looking like a mermaid out of water. I would frequently daydream about it. In my fantasy I'd walk into the room, and everyone would be entranced by my beauty. I would look tall and regal and intensely exotic. My eyes would crinkle with delight, and I would be both beloved and desired in the most provocative way. Every night for weeks, I lay in bed with YouTube makeup tutorials playing in the background on my phone and replaying how the night would go.

I wasn't educated in the signs of mania during my short stint as someone diagnosed with bipolar disorder back in my twenties. Depression was easier for me to feel, and I wasn't told that I could experience mixed episodes of depression and mania at the same time. During these mixed episodes I would get so fixated on the depression that I could not even see the bizarre manifestations of mania happening in my life.

My mania in those last days of sanity included obsessively photographing women posing in the roots of trees for a photography project I was working on. Once, when I got a haircut, before the stylist could wash it she had to pull out a pile of small twigs and leaves from the nest that was my hair. The photographs I captured during that time are haunting, deep with emotion. I was sure they would be displayed in a large downtown gallery. I would wear a floor-length, modern, blue and grey gown, and everyone would love me.

I also compulsively shopped online and stayed up nearly all night most nights. For months I would be up for five to six hours after Noah went to bed. I was frantic and so alone it felt like I would suffocate. One such desperate night, while scrolling my phone for worthiness and an exit from the pain, I happened upon a makeup tutorial filmed by a woman with a southern drawl. I never wore makeup, and something about her voice drew me in, soothed me. It brought me relief, like fresh air, for a few glorious minutes. This quickly escalated to obsession: I watched and listened to make up videos throughout the day—while driving, while editing my roots photos, and during my late-night bath. I would watch them for hours before finally falling to sleep.

I was the heaviest I had ever been. I had not realized how big I had gotten because I could only see myself as what I felt I was—tall, regal, able to effortlessly converse with and charm people. A vision.

On the day of the fundraiser I was photographing a family for my part time job. They lived in a nearby city that had a Sephora makeup store. Never in my life had I graced the doors of a makeup store, but as soon as the photo session was over, I ran inside, full of energy and ideas, and said to the first makeup lady I could find, "I'm going to a ball tonight, and I want to look like a mermaid!" I must have looked and sounded ridiculous. That beautiful black woman didn't miss a beat, and soon my basket was full of sparkly blues, greens, and coral. She hooked me up with everything I could need, and I bought it all—two hundred dollars' worth of makeup. When I got home, I didn't know where to put it since up to then I owned exactly one tube of mascara that stood upright next to my toothpaste. I got to work doing all the things I'd seen done on the YouTube tutorials: foundation over my beautiful freckles, coral blush to add a hint of the flush that I had just covered up, eyeliner in vivid green, eye shadows in glittery blues and greens, a thick application of mascara. I slipped on my dress with nothing to hold my flesh in underneath it and blow-dried my long hair till it was almost dry. I was feeling incredible. Unlike the wind, this vision was coming to life.

When we arrived, I stepped out of our friend's truck and onto the lush, green lawn and someone snapped a picture of Noah and me. I stood tall while my heels sunk into the earth. Smile and click. Before walking up to the country clubhouse, I glanced at the picture and all at once, everything shattered like broken glass. I looked lumpy, vacant, and dead. I looked like a painted freak. I barely made it through the door before frantically searching for a bathroom. Inside the stall, I slid down the wall to the floor in defeat. Tears streamed down my face and all over my sparkling dress, leaving streaks of black and green on my painted cheeks. I went over to the sink, wet a paper towel, and started wiping it all away, angry that I could be so stupid. Noah must have been too distracted and too uneducated about make up to notice. How could I not see this before I left the house?

After wiping all of it off, I joined the crowd outside and sat on an elaborate love seat at the back of the bar, my head bowed in shame. I noticed the muted, conservative dresses on the other women. Black shift dresses, beige dinner jackets, and lots of pants suits. I glanced down at the golden gown that clung to every bump of my thighs. Back to the bathroom I went. I stared at my reflection, at my washed-out face, and felt such disgust that my stomach turned. Several times throughout the night I would leave my jolly group of friends and return to lie on the floor at the base of the toilet, sobbing silently. I would splash cold water on my face to relieve my puffy red eyes and go back out there again. Between trips to the bathroom floor, I drank so much that the evening was a blur. I went to bed with thoughts of suicide swirling around my head and a drawer full of mermaid makeup I would never use again.

THE MASK

I wear a mask.

Not by choice.

Sometimes it melts onto my face

Like butter on a warm piece of toast.

Sometimes it is calloused like armor.

My cheeks are plump and tight,

Giving the illusion that I'm always smiling,

Even if my heart is breaking.

My eyes naturally crinkle like I'm delighted.

Mostly I am.

But when I'm not, they betray me.

My heart longs to be authentic,

But this mask serves as a thick shroud.

When I try to tell people, they don't believe me.

"You can't be sad. You're Helen Joy!"

"But you look happy every day."

I long to take it off.

I long to be seen.

THE WALKING CORPSE

The fall of 2016 was what I call my muddy period—mania mixed with depression. Like a pendulum, I was swinging constantly from one to the other, and no matter how hard I tried I couldn't stay anchored in the center. My mind was racing and groggy at the same time. It kept filling with thoughts on how to live a better life—thoughts that kept threatening to erupt from me like a giant volcano. One morning, overwhelmed, I ran to my bed, grabbed my journal, and flopped on my belly, prepared to take the time—hours if I needed it—to pour out every thought from my head, emptying it like a pitcher of water. I scribbled:

Steps (tiny steps) to living your dream:

1. Brush your teeth.

2. Read to the children.

Then I went blank. I stared at the pages for ten minutes and couldn't get another thing out. I knew that I couldn't even follow a two-step process to achieve my dreams, not even when it came to brushing my teeth. I was running around like crazy but wasn't accomplishing the simplest of tasks. I would go to Earth Fare and fill my cart with beautiful organic produce and healthy snacks, feeling like I was coming up for air. I would look down into my cart and feel so proud. I was going to crawl out of this pit of darkness, and a spaghetti squash would be the catalyst to bring me back to my former glory. No one in the entire world wanted to be better more than me. No one strived harder. Yet that squash rotted in my kitchen.

My skin started to feel like it was burning. The last time I nursed Lucy, we were reclining in a warm bath like we had done a hundred times. But this time, when she latched on it felt like I was burning wherever her body came in contact with my skin. I quickly pulled her off of me and stared at her in shock. Something had changed deep inside of me, something I didn't like.

For months I had steadily gotten heavier, slower, sleepier. I felt like people didn't like me, that they actually hated to be in my presence. I was deeply paranoid. My marriage was painful. Every marriage counseling session seemed like it ended in defeat.

It felt like I was living behind that same piece of dirty glass, looking through it at all the happy life going on around me and being unable to participate. I felt so alone, so separate. Whenever I spoke to someone, I felt like they couldn't hear me. I was asking for help, and they were saying, "Why don't you just go to bed earlier? You won't be so tired." They told me I wasn't eating the right foods, or that I was watching the wrong things on TV. "Why don't you just read your Bible?" "Just walk! Just pray!" "You need vitamin D; go outside." "God is teaching you something; He won't give you more than you can handle."

This unhelpful advice only heaped hot coals of guilt onto my head and transmitted shame to every inch of my being. I wasn't enough; I was lazy and stupid and obviously not doing the right things for even God to hear my cries.

For months, at church every Sunday I stared at the blue chairs in front of me, unthinking, unblinking, staring at the backs of the people raising their hands or singing with joy. I used to feel like that. I used to be awake and bursting with life, but now there were no songs in my heart. I couldn't sing. I couldn't even stand.

One dark Sunday in November, I came to church a walking corpse, violin dangling from my arm. My body felt heavy, my mind felt delirious with invisible, psychic pain. I was frantic, searching for a way out, and prayed that being in that holy building would provide me with answers. Even though I had felt dead to things of God for months, that day the lyrics of a song we played penetrated my mind and my soul, bringing hope.

Rock of ages, when the day seems long,

From this labor and this heartache I have come.

The skies will wear out, but you remain the same: Rock of Ages, I praise your name.

Rock of Ages, you have brought me near,

You have poured out your lifeblood, your love, your tears

To make this stone heart come alive again,

Rock of Ages, forgive my sin.

I swayed to the music and played that song on my violin with tears pouring down my face. It was mournful. I was clinging to it like it was the last thin root hanging over a deep ravine.

That month the mountains were covered in smothering smoke from nearby wildfires. It was hard to breathe, it was so thick. Donald Trump had won the presidential election, and all the negative feelings worldwide seemed to target my body. After church, Noah decided that it would be a family day. As my family scurried around gathering items to go on an adventure, I sat in the passenger's side of the car, limp as a rag doll. I had poured out every bit of energy at church. It felt excruciating to think of putting on my own seatbelt. I didn't help anyone get ready. I just sat quietly, tears spilling over as we drove to the next town up. The boys went to a pinball museum, and I took Lucy to the mall where we wandered aimlessly and didn't buy anything, then we all got tacos together. I sobbed throughout the whole meal, and Noah was annoyed that I couldn't get it together. On the way home, I tried to reach him through the thick glass that separated us. I tried to let him know how bad things were. He couldn't hear me, even if I shouted.

My light, which used to shine so brightly, had for years been reduced to flickering. That night it was finally extinguished. There would be no more striving. Suicide seemed a reality. As Noah and I got into bed, I was shaking with grief, desperate to be held. Instead, we had an argument. I made a last-ditch effort to be seen in the dark. Did Noah see any light in me at all?

"I feel like I'm dying. I feel like I'm dying! Why won't you help me? Why won't you love me?" I screamed as I beat my fists on our headboard. But his own pain and fear of me was so vast, he shut down and turned his back to sleep. I writhed around in our bed, clawing at the sheets and moaning like a woman about to give birth. The hurt was eating me alive.

In the wee morning hours I opened my phone and emailed our marriage counselor, Brian, who I usually felt connected to but recently felt had faded away just like everyone else. "I'm not sure if I can do this.

I feel like I'm dying of a broken heart. I feel abandoned by Noah, by you, by friends that I've reached out to. I don't know if I've expressed how urgent this is. I know you said I need to be patient, but I don't know if I can be. I think I will just die of sadness." There would be no reply, because everyone was sleeping. As I tried to fall asleep, I watched my vacant eyes in the mirror across from my bed, slipping down, down, down, under the cold, deep water.

FIRST DAY

The next morning was a cold, frigid day, and I was sorry I woke up. I was sorry I was breathing. As I lay in bed, my phone flashed with an email back from Brian, saying that if I wanted to meet that day it would need to be at his house, since it was his day off. We were friends with his family from church and his wife, Katie, and their kids would be there. I couldn't imagine bringing my grief into their home and quickly replied, "No thanks." He wrote back and said he could sneak me in through the garage so that their children wouldn't even know I was there. I reluctantly agreed.

That I could step out of bed that morning was a miracle. I clumsily packed my children's lunches with leftover scraps. I had recently stopped grocery shopping after months of spending hundreds of dollars on food I would never cook. I sent my boys to school without kissing them goodbye and drove Lucy to preschool in the clothes both of us had worn the day before. My hair was unbrushed and slightly matted. Several other mothers asked me how I was that morning, and I straight-faced lied. "Fine. Good."

Fifteen minutes later Katie led me into the basement of their home. I collapsed onto the floor at the foot of their couch. This was not drama, this was agony. I saw in their eyes that they saw me; someone finally saw me. Katie brought me tea and rubbed my back. I lay my head down as I wept, right on their thick, fringe carpet. I don't really remember what I said, babbling on about my marriage and how I couldn't make it one more day the way things were. As I talked, Brian's eyes changed in a way I had never seen. After a few minutes of listening, he said gently, "Helen Joy, I know you don't want to do this, but I think you might actually need to get some serious help. I think you might need to go to a hospital today. I can make you go, or you can decide to take yourself on your own."

The thought that I could get professional help had never crossed my mind, and now I was hearing that I could finally get relief from the horror show that had become my life. My brain was going a mile a minute, and I was so tired. All I could think about was a bed. I wanted to sleep. I didn't think about my kids. I didn't think about my husband. The only person I thought about was my friend Catherine, who was due any day with her first baby and whose birth I had planned to attend since before this baby was conceived. I glanced down at my phone, and at that very second up popped a text from her, telling me the doctor said she had not yet dilated and delivery was still far off. I handed my phone to Katie and said, "Take me."

It felt like it always did when I decided to go to the hospital to deliver a baby. Once I made up my mind, the pain disappeared for a second, then adrenaline started pumping and everything became surreal. I was shaking like mad when I handed over my keys and climbed into the passenger seat of my van. Brian drove, and I went numb. Blank. He called Noah to let him know the situation. He called Summer. I couldn't hear their responses. I was adamant that my mom not know, because I knew she'd want to take care of me and I knew it wouldn't help. As we drove along, I began to think about what it would be like at the hospital. I was under the impression that I would get checked in, spend two or three days resting, and maybe get on some meds. Maybe they could help me sleep and I would finally feel better. Throughout the drive, Brian told me he was proud of me, and I felt nothing. Only a pounding in my head.

When we got to the hospital, I put my wedding ring in the glove compartment of the van for safekeeping, and we headed in. I felt so light, like baggage had been cut away from my body. I had made the right decision.

It's pretty uncomfortable to have to go into the intimate details of how you wanted to end your life to three different nurses three different times while everyone in the emergency room is staring at you. I was crying and making strange, animalistic sounds. Brian was kind and comforting as we waited. My mom-brain abruptly kicked in, and while we waited I started dictating to Brian tasks for Noah to do while I was gone. Pay this bill, call this guy, find someone to get the boys from school. Brian texted him. Noah was confused by why I was thinking about these things when I supposedly wanted to die. I can't explain it; brains just work that way.

Thankfully, I didn't have to linger in the waiting room long before they took me back to be admitted. In a tiny utility closet filled with cleaning supplies, I was made to strip in front of a female nurse. She checked every inch of me, and I sensed she felt bad about it. She gave me extra-large men's green paper scrubs. They fit my hips but were about eight inches too long. My breasts hung down, and I felt exposed to have only paper between me and the world. I was led through a dark corridor, rustling conspicuously along while passing eerie, glowing squares of windows on each door. The windows peered into tiny rooms with one bed. It was exactly what I thought it would be like. As soon as they left me in my room, my body gave up control, I collapsed on the bed, and collapsed into sleep.

I was disturbed out of a vivid dream just a few minutes later by more questions and pokes. The sickening, sterile smell reminded me of those months visiting my father in the hospital. My head was pounding with a migraine, and I didn't know how long it had been since I had eaten anything. It is surprisingly hard to get ibuprofen for a headache in a hospital. Men outside my little window were banging on the nurses station demanding narcotics, but ibuprofen proved to be just as hard to get. After waiting for hours, I got up the courage to ask for some food. They brought a grilled chicken sandwich that I devoured even though the lettuce was wilted and the bun was soggy with mayonnaise, which I hate.

I heard screaming. I heard people being forcefully brought in by police. I quietly sank into the thin mattress, hoping no one would see me, hoping that I wouldn't be grouped with them. A thin black man was running laps in the hall, and every few minutes he would stop and pop his head in my window, wide-eyed and demented. His white teeth glowed in the darkness. He stared at me and I at him. It felt like he was hungry and wanted to eat me.

I found out that this unit, which felt contained and safe, was not where I would be staying. This was just a holding pen in the ER while the insane waited for beds elsewhere. Hours ticked by, and a bed finally became available. I was prepped to be transferred. An armed guard escorted me out of the hospital, through the same doors I had walked through to deliver two of my babies. I was wearing socks with sticky spots on the bottom, and my green paper pants rustled and dragged the ground as people stared. I looked and felt like a prisoner. I was loaded into a van with bulletproof glass dividing me from the driver and was driven across the busy street to another part of the hospital. The smoke from the fires was thick as they unloaded me, turning me over to a young, Hispanic male nurse. While walking me down the hall he said in a chipper voice, "How's your day going?" I stared at him with dead eyes; I couldn't believe I was having to answer this question here. "It's actually my worst day ever," I replied. He dropped his head and walked the rest of the distance in silence. I think of him sometimes, and I bet you he's not asking patients entering the psych unit how their days are going anymore. Maybe that was his first day.

When I walked into the unit I left my mask at the door and entered raw and utterly myself. For the first time in my whole life I could act exactly how I felt. I didn't smile for three days. Not once. It felt so good to finally feel what my body had been telling me for years. That I was not okay.

The whole evening played out like a bad movie. People were screaming and yelling, making my still-aching head throb. They put me in a small room, separated from the chaos by just a thin blue curtain. No one checked on me for hours. My bed was near the common area and directly across from the only patient telephone. I lay in bed listening to the turmoil: people demanding drugs and yelling, psychotic people,

people that weren't like me. I started panicking; I had made a terrible mistake. I surely did not belong there.

I was longing for some peppermint oil, which had soothed my migraines since I was a child. I threw up from the pain and was desperate for relief, so I took the small tube of toothpaste they gave me and rubbed it into my temples. It didn't help. One nurse finally took pity on me and brought me bags of ice and then bags of heated-up wet washcloths to try to help. No one would give me a high dose of ibuprofen to make it go away. They were acting like I was asking for street drugs.

I finally fell into a fitful sleep, hoping the nightmare would be over when I woke up. A little before midnight I was abruptly pulled from my bed by a male nurse who took me into a room with just a monitor on a rolling table and a chair. A doctor talked to me through the monitor. It was a video conference of sorts. He was distracted and distant and looked like he had just come off of a twelve-hour shift. He asked me general questions, and I don't remember what I said. I cried. A lot. I don't know how he could even hear me through my sobs. After a time, I was escorted back to my bed, where I tried again for hours to slip back into sleep.

Tossing on my mattress, I thought, *This has to be a nightmare. Tomorrow, surely, I will be comforted.*

SECOND DAY

"Obama put a microchip in my arm! I tried to gnaw it out! My arm's bleeding! I need stitches!" The yelling of the woman down the hall woke me early the next morning. The nurses ignored her. "Don't get near me with your cell phones or electronics, they'll zap me. They'll zap me! Why won't you get me an MRI so I can surgically remove it?"

What had I done? Who was taking care of my children? Who was going to go to their Thanksgiving lunch at school? I didn't belong here with this crazy woman. I felt sick. I had to get out of there as soon as possible.

I lay still in my cot, staring up at my reflection in the ceiling light. All I could see were my legs curled up in the fetal position, the pink, kidney-shaped plastic container that housed my soap and toothbrush, and the shape of my comb on the floor. It was a strange scene; it felt like I was looking at someone else.

I listened to the commotion outside my room, still as a mouse, curious yet terrified. A woman with a strong southern accent was demanding narcotics to crush and snort. Another several curtains over was screaming "cunt" to the female doctor. My stomach recoiled. Everyone was demanding something. Everyone but me. My needs felt laughable and trite.

I slipped out of my bed to the phone outside my curtain and dialed Brian. My hair hung down over my face, and I didn't look at anyone as I whispered into the phone. I told him no one was helping me. He said he would do all he could do from the outside to get me help.

I was shaking as I dialed Summer. I didn't know what I would say, I just wanted to hear a friendly voice. I don't know what either of us ended up talking about, except that she told me she had come straight to the waiting room at the ER and waited for hours, even though she knew she couldn't see me. I clung to that. I couldn't bring myself to call Noah, so I slipped back into my room, unsure of what I was waiting for. It was then that I learned something awful. I was not even in the actual psych unit; this was called psych holding (where I thought I had been originally), and it housed the overflow until people could be discharged or sent upstairs to the regular psych ward. I looked around. Why was I here? Why was I here with these crazy people? I just wanted to sleep a little, I just wanted my manic thoughts to stop, I just wanted to stay alive.

I felt completely invisible for hours. Finally, a heavyset, male nurse came and told me it was my turn for a shower. I was relieved for the distraction. He guided me to the one shower on the unit, and I was given fresh paper clothes and two towels. There was no lock on the door. I lay my towels down on the bottom of the shower, curled up on them, and cried as the hot water pounded the fear out of my body. Afterwards, still soaking wet, I put on the baggy paper scrubs and went to the nurses station in the middle of the unit. I meekly asked if my husband could bring me a book and a bra and was told no, I had to wait till I got upstairs.

On the way back to my room, I passed by a leaning shelf apparently meant to house books, games, and art supplies for the unit. It held just three books, two board games with only a few pieces each, a cat puzzle that I was certain did not contain all the pieces, and a few tattered coloring books but nothing to color with. I grabbed all three books and returned to my room.

The first one I opened was a 1984 children's book about the Olympics. It was an old library book and had that musty smell and that clear, shiny plastic cover protector. It was about thirty pages long. I read every word three times and looked at all the pictures. Before I knew it, I had memorized the book from cover to cover. The next one was a 1984 children's book called *Ice Dancing.* I did the same thing—read it front to back three times. I peeked at the clock. Only twenty minutes had gone by. The third book was a biography of Tom Cruise, written in German. I cracked it open to look at the photographs in the middle. Hand-drawn on the pictures were nasty words, phallic symbols, and swastikas. That was the extent of the library, and it had taken up only twenty-four minutes of my day. I took the books back to their place and was instantly swarmed by patients curious about me.

"Why are you here?" they asked with morbid curiosity.

"I'm just really sad," I answered, not wanting to tell them about my flirtation with suicide.

It was odd to be the sad girl. I was used to being Helen Joy, living up to my name. But it felt good to be sad out loud.

A nurse came by to take my vitals, and I asked him when a doctor would see me so I could go home to my children. He told me I had to wait for a bed and was kind enough to print twenty pages of word searches for me from the nurses station computer. I lay on my stomach doing them while listening through my sheer curtain to the chaos outside.

Microchip lady called her husband twenty times in a row, giving him links to YouTube videos that would convince him the government was out to get her. She believed Trump was bringing a new solar system down to the earth to save the world's population. and she needed to recruit people to help. Later she stuck her head in my room and asked me what my job was. I told her I was an artist. She was pleased and told me I was now in charge of designing posters announcing the new solar system. The corners of my lips turned up just slightly. I was fascinated that a brain could fragment like that.

I watched the walkers in their teal sticky socks that squeaked the slightest bit as they did laps around the ward for hours. There was a middle-aged man with a childlike demeanor. I never heard him speak one word till the end of my stay when they were dragging him out the door and he exploded with a barrage of curse words. There was a young boy who was detoxing from alcohol and was in so much pain. He called his mom several times, begging her for a second chance, pleading for a ride home. She said no. I guess his luck had finally run dry. Then there was a young homeless boy with a sweet southern drawl but the eyes of someone who lived in hell. Round and round they walked, and I hung onto every word I could hear.

By the afternoon I was feeling desperate to get out. Maybe these people didn't have families waiting for them at home, but I sure did. I wasn't like them, and I didn't know why I was locked up with them. I became so homesick that I got up the courage to call Noah. I tried to tune out the confusion of his voice and the ache I felt for our children. I had to shut it down. I told him he could tell my mom where I was.

That afternoon they brought in Jim. Jim was an enormously large man with two black eyes from being beaten up. His large stomach hung low between his legs, and I could see every part of him through his thin paper scrubs. Once, he leaned back and stretched the pants tight with his hands to show me his penis. "Look at this," he grunted, looking me straight in the eyes. He was so close he could have touched me. He was vile, but he thought highly of himself and talked constantly about how good he was compared to other men. How good he loved his women. He talked real slow and called me sweetheart. His job on the outside was helping out at a halfway house, and he had trouble sleeping. He had taken a whole bottle of something to sleep, and that was why he was here. One moment Jim was sickly sweet and gentle, then he would suddenly become violent and demanding. He wanted stronger drugs for his head from the beating and thrashed around breaking things because he couldn't get them. In the middle of the night he pulled down the curtain in the room next to me. He also pulled his pants down to the nurses.

Every night I would hear Jim call his online girlfriend and describe in vivid detail what he wanted to do to her sexually—graphic, disturbing details that I will never utter out loud. At the end of his calls he would announce loudly how he was unable to stand up and how he needed to go take a shower to "take care of it." This is precisely the reason I didn't use my towels to dry off but instead stood on them in the shower. Several times, Jim told me he was going to sneak into my bed at night, and I believed he would. I was terrified, and I was trapped. I was sure

I would be raped in the very facility where I had committed myself to stay safe. I still have nightmares about Jim. Once, while shopping at a store, I saw the back of a massive man, just his height and girth, and swore I heard Jim's honey-sweet voice. I ran to the bathroom and locked myself in, collapsing onto the dirty floor, shaking with fright. After ten minutes I got the courage to come out. It wasn't even him.

At mealtime the nurses would throw open my curtain, and all the patients in their green paper scrubs would stare at me, morbidly curious, because I stayed hidden in my room. I watched several homeless men start grabbing handfuls of food and hiding them in their scrubs. One approached me when he saw I wasn't eating my meat and asked if he could take it. He stared at me with his sunken eyes and told me he liked to load up when he was there. I told him to have at it, so he stuck his hand in my food and took it away to his room. I thought this type of thing only happened in prison TV shows. I couldn't believe it was happening to me, a white suburban mom.

I lay in bed late at night, trying to fall asleep despite the glow of the fluorescent lights in the hallway. An ugly monster started to overtake me. It squeezed me until I could barely catch my breath. Why was no one seeing me? Why was no one helping me? Did I need to tear down a curtain and take my pants off to be seen?

Close to midnight, I asked a pretty, young nurse with chin-length dark hair to come to my temporary room. She stood in the corner, her face lit by the glowing monitor, and I lost it.

"Why won't anyone help me? Why am I still here? I wanted to die before I came in, and now I want to die more. How can you let this happen? Save me! Please save me!"

As I sobbed, she backed into the corner, her face blank and uncaring. She stayed there, staring at me. "My hands are tied," she finally said, and she left me there.

I imagine that nurse had started her career with a nurturing heart and a desire to help people. Now she was worn down by the system, by the red tape. I was one of a thousand faces she had to leave behind.

I spent the next hours writhing around on my mattress, crying out to God. Because we were not allowed to have fitted sheets for safety reasons, my flat sheet slipped off and I was left on the bare, aging, plastic mattress that had housed thousands of bodies. It was wet from my tears, and eventually, after I had cried every last drop that was inside of me, I surrendered to it.

NATIVE AMERICAN WOMAN

I've heard stories of the ways that humans cope with extreme pressure, loneliness, or pain. Stories of pretending to eat a meal when they're starving, imagining a warm fire when it's freezing outside. This type of thing happened to me on that second night after the nurse left me writhing in pain.

I thought I would die from loneliness, from lack of compassion. I needed to be nurtured to live, I needed to be touched. So my brain created a place for that to happen.

I open my eyes to a pair of soft, brown eyes looking into mine. They are gentle and loving, overflowing with compassion, but not pity. They belong to a wrinkled Native American woman who is curled up next to me, hand in my hair, stroking it just like my mama used to. Her eyes are telling me two things, without any words.

"I am here."

"You will live."

We are lying in a nest of soft wool next to a cozy fire that is casting lovely warm shadows all around me. We are in a wigwam with two other nests of women being taken care of, being nursed back to living. She feeds me broth, she gives me tea, she brushes the hair off of my face so tenderly. Every time I feel scared, she looks at me.

"*I am here. I am here,*" *her eyes assure me.*

When I'm not in blissful sleep, we walk together next to the river, which is separated from the wigwam by a clear fence to make me feel safe. I breathe in the life-giving air. I'm not trapped. I'm not alone.

She sees me. She doesn't try to fix me. She's here. She's just here.

THIRD DAY

I woke up the third day determined to get the hell out of there. In the time since I had been admitted, others had come and gone while I was left with the forgotten. I had never done drugs or gone to jail, I had a family ready to care for me on the outside, and I was left with these neglected people who were in no hurry to leave. Many of them had come in off the streets for food and warmth, and they were just fine staying there as long as the system would allow. Others were completely out of their minds, and I don't think it even mattered to them where they were.

The doctor all the patients called Dr. Cunt finally came to talk to me. She was a worn woman with stringy blond hair, and her eyes looked like she was being hunted. Without even questioning me, she told me they were going to put me on the same medication I had been given in college, the same dosage. She also told me I would not get a bed in the actual psych ward because I did not have health insurance. I couldn't believe it. I was part of a network of Christians who sent checks to help cover other people's medical expenses, but that meant nothing here. As her words sank in, I began to think that maybe I would be stuck there forever, lost in the bowels of the hospital.

Dread consumed me, followed quickly by determination. I started frantically making phone calls. Brian dictated numbers for surrounding hospitals, and I wrote them on my arm. I called each one, and each one immediately hung up when I mentioned I was a patient across town. Except for one woman who listened for a minute until I told her my husband would bring cash that day so that they would be paid. Then she hung up. I even tried calling 911 and was hung up on.

I was panicked, stuck, and feeling worse every minute. I should never have done this. I should have gone to my mom's house and let her tie me to a bed to keep me from dying. That would be better than this.

Then an angel came into my room—an angel with compassion in his eyes, and I knew immediately that he saw me. He saw my need and my humanity. He was a social worker who told me it could be days before a place opened up for me because of the insurance. He encouraged me to come out of my room and interact with the other patients so maybe I could be released to get treatment outside of the hospital. I was on it. I put my good-girl mask back on and headed out to socialize.

Crazy microchip lady came up to me after breakfast, propped her leg up on a chair, and started inhaling a used tampon applicator covered in blood like it was a Cuban cigar. She kept this up while she told me more about the chip in her arm. "Ya know when you go to your refrigerator and open the vegetable drawer and there's a bunch of severed heads in it?"

"Um, no, that's never happened to me."

Puff, puff, exhale.

"Well if you don't watch out, they're coming for you." Blood had gathered in the corners of her mouth, and I tried not to vomit.

I visited with the soft-spoken homeless boy. He was about twenty-four and had been homeless for years. His speech slurred with every sentence, a result of years of drug and alcohol abuse. His stories tortured my heart. He grew up in the back woods, where his dad taught him to huff gas at the age of five and injected him with drugs. He never had a chance. He was addicted to anything that numbed him out. He called me Helen and was fascinated that I didn't do drugs of any kind, questioning me like one would question a celebrity. When I told him I was a mom, he was amazed. He thought I was a teenager. He told me he once got high with a woman while her three small children were sleeping. When he woke up, the mom was gone and he took care of those children until she returned a week later, doing the best he could. He told me he knew being a mom was hard work.

A year later, I saw him downtown begging for money as I was running to a dinner reservation at a fancy restaurant. I rounded up twenty dollars to take back to him, even though I knew what he would buy with it. I just wanted him to know I remembered his name and that I cared for him. He was gone before I returned. I think of him nearly every day.

These people were in no hurry to leave. It was bitter cold outside, and most of them didn't have homes. Surely they didn't have insurance either. They couldn't understand my urgency to get out. I couldn't stand the thought of getting lumped in with them. The forgotten. The unlovable. The forever broken.

That day dragged on forever, just like the two before. I would make pointless calls that got me nowhere, then I would attempt to complete the puzzle with missing pieces with my new "friends." I tried to act happier; I tried to give the staff what they wanted to see.

That night, as I was trying to fall asleep, all the men in the unit, led by Jim, gathered outside my room in the common area. They huddled and talked in disgusting detail about their girlfriends' bodies—how they looked, how they felt, how they smelled, how they tasted, how it felt to be inside of them. I felt sick and feverish. As each of them shared, moans would come from the others. I felt like I could hear them licking their lips. I was embarrassed and ashamed that I could hear them, so I snuck out to ask the nurse if they had any earplugs. She gave me a pair, and I pushed them into my ears and pulled my pillow on top of my head, but I could still hear those men. It seemed like they got louder, and no part of me felt worthy of asking them to stop. I was not a person in there. When I asked for help, no one helped me.

Every time I fell asleep, I awoke to anarchy—to security guards dragging people away; to screaming, yelling, things crashing. One woman called 911, and the police actually showed up. I swore on my life that night that if I got out, I was going straight to the media. What was happening there was illegal, inhumane, and I would stop it. We were humans! We were humans! It had to be stopped.

That hospital stay was the most horrific experience I'd ever had. It not only stripped me of my dignity and my humanity, but it took away whatever innocence I had left—and that's something I can never get back.

FOURTH DAY

I awoke with a start, with a desperate need to survive and escape. I was in fight or flight mode with no ability to fly. I could not spend one more night in there. I needed touch, I needed love, and it wasn't coming through the phone outside of my room. It became clear that even though I didn't feel better, I had to put my mask on again to get out.

Since I'd been there, different social workers had spoken with me twice each day. The meetings were brief and not helpful except with the one man who saw me. I awaited each session anxiously, pacing back and forth in my room, dragging my fingertips along the blue curtain.

The social workers were defeated. They were defeated before they ever walked into my room. I imagined them fresh out of college with a vision and a passion to help people, just like the nurse two nights before. Red tape had worn them down too. Their eyes were deep pools of sadness, but I could still see sparks of compassion. They wanted to help but, despite their good hearts, their hands were tied. There were too many people and not enough resources.

I remember the social worker that last day like I remember my mama's face. His large body filled the corner of my room, and his tough exterior melted as I pleaded my case. I purposefully exuded wisdom and warmth while inside I was raging with panic. I told him I was feeling better and ready to join my incredible support system on the outside. I told him I would be a five-star student, go to therapy whenever they asked, and take the meds prescribed. I told him I could give him a list of people who would hold me accountable. The mask did its job, as it had done my whole life.

After conferring with the people above him, the social worker came back to tell me they would discharge me—against medical advice—that day. I held my breath until he left my room. As soon as I let the air from my lungs, I was flooded with relief, with grief from being away from my children, and with desperation to be wrapped up in the arms of someone who loved me.

As the nurses were getting ready to discharge me, a bed became available in a hospital an hour and a half away, and the social worker told me I could be transported later that day.

No, no, no, no, no! I'm about to break free! I cannot go to another hell like this. My heart was beating fast, but the mask held steady.

Gritting my teeth and smiling, I said, "I don't want to do the wrong thing, but I really think it's best for me to be with my family, you know? I'm feeling so much better. I really think I'll be fine to go home."

Please work. Please work. Please work, I chanted inside.

Once more, he agreed to let me go, although he warned me sternly about how serious it was to refuse medical care.

He left, the mask fell again, and I cried and prayed and thanked God while quietly jumping up and down. I did it! I called Noah and told him he could finally come and get me.

I hate hospital time. Minutes take hours, and hours crawl by like days. I sat outside my room and let the bustle surround me like I was the eye of a hurricane. The walkers in their sticky socks, the patients banging on the glass of the nurses station, and the chatter—it all became a droning noise to me. I pulled and scratched at my skin, eyeing the locked exit door, and the minutes ticked by. Jim was finally moved to the psych unit, and I felt safe for the first time in days.

To my great relief, someone found eight crayons somewhere, and the nurses gave us some paper to draw on. I sat around the table with the unlovable, the forgotten, the insane, and we drew.

At last, it was my turn to leave. I was shaking like I was when I had come in. They handed me a bag of my things: my dress, my worn-out slippers, and my underwear. Humanity in a bag. As I stood there in my clothes, surrounded by everyone in green paper, my new friends said their goodbyes. One woman gave me her number to tuck into my bra.

I asked for my prescription for the medication I had been given the day before, but they told me that because I was discharging against medical advice, they couldn't give it to me. I froze. That wasn't the plan. I felt myself slipping again. *Keep the mask on, keep the mask on.* I could see my freedom, almost touch it, but all the damn rules were stopping me from grabbing it. Then they told me I had an appointment at eight o'clock the next morning with a psychiatrist who could give me a prescription. I started to breathe again. I would be okay after all. Still, deep down, a small voice told me I wouldn't be.

The nurse led me out into the biting cold, and I didn't even mind it. The sun, the sounds, the air—they welcomed me back into the world with a tender embrace. The nurse and I waited and waited for Noah to pull up. When he didn't come, I thought maybe I would start running down the road as fast as I could. But I waited, arms crossed, heart pounding. He finally pulled up to the curb. I greeted him with smiles, a hug, and a kiss on his cheek. We signed some papers, I crawled into my beloved, messy van, and they let me go.

The second we left that place I ripped the mask off. I didn't cry; instead, I started yelling. "We have to tell someone! We have to tell someone that they treat people like animals in there!" I wanted to go to the news station. I wanted to tell the police. The savageness of that place was hard to fathom, and I knew that no matter what I said, no one, no one would know. Noah drove in silence. I could feel his fear.

When we pulled up to our home I was overwhelmed with how big it was, how full of comforting, beautiful things it was. I was overwhelmed with the books I could read and the music I could listen to. It had only been four days, but if you've ever had your humanity stripped from you, the daily things you take for granted become the very things you cherish the most.

I was anxious to see my kids but nervous. I had changed inside. Would they notice? Would they be scared of me? I felt tainted by everything I had witnessed, all the ugliness that I had no choice but to breathe in. No one had told my kids what had happened, so when they saw me they didn't even stop their coloring and just said, "How was your trip, Mama?"

My sister Julianna, who had driven five hours with a toddler and a big belly of baby the minute she heard about me, brought a pot of soup my mama had made for me. I didn't want to see Mom. I couldn't fathom handling the emotions I knew would spill from her. I needed calm. I needed steady. I couldn't take in an ounce of anyone else's pain. I ate the soup like I was eating pure love. But it curdled in my stomach, and I was sick.

I was so tired. Tired in my bones. I had lain in a bed for days, and still I was aching for rest. When I climbed into our bed, which was messy, soft, and smelled like sweat, Noah held me close in a way he never had. But I still didn't feel comforted, I still didn't feel safe. As his breathing slowed and relaxed, the horrors of the darkness overtook me. I was suffocating again. Tears fell down my cheeks as I stared at my reflection in the same mirror I had looked in five days earlier. I wasn't better; I was worse. My lifeline of the psychiatrist was ten hours away. If I could get there, maybe someone would finally see me and help me.

SHE SAID MY NAME

The taste of vomit woke me up, and I was sick for twenty minutes. While Noah took the kids to school, I hurriedly threw on a dress and slippers and drove to the local government office for my eight o'clock appointment, shaking the whole time. I tried to open the door of the beige building, but it was locked up tight. The sign on the door said that the place didn't open for another half hour. Panic rose in my chest, bringing me close to puking again. They forgot my appointment! It felt like all of my blood drained from my body. I made three frantic calls and left three desperate messages, hoping someone would reassure me that I would be seen that day, that I would get care.

I paced for thirty minutes outside the office, wringing my hands. *It's going to be okay. It's going to be okay.* I had developed a full-blown migraine by this point and was reeling from the pounding in my head. It reminded me of that first day I committed myself.

At eight thirty someone unlocked the door. I burst inside and started begging, "Please! Please! I had an eight a.m. appointment. I don't know what happened. Can you still see me?"

The woman at the desk was unkind and robotlike, desensitized from years of seeing people like me. "We don't do appointments; it's a walk-in clinic," she flatly responded.

The waiting room was yellow and old. It smelled like cigarettes and musty carpet, which I was pretty sure hadn't been changed or cleaned since the seventies. Men poured in around me, men who reminded me of the place I had just escaped—rough, dirty, and hopeless. I sensed them undressing me with their eyes. My skin crawled, and I wanted to run out into the fresh air. Instead, I rocked back and forth in my chair, anxiously waiting for them to call my name. Tears dripped down my face. I was afraid. I was so afraid. Finally, they called my name.

A slow-moving older woman took me to a room in the back. She introduced me to a high schooler who was shadowing her that month for a senior project. The teenager smiled brightly and asked how I was doing. I lay my head down on the table and said, "I don't want to live anymore. I need help." I was asked all sorts of intimate questions in front of this idealistic teenager; her eyes grew wide as I described in detail the horrors of the hospital and my growing desire to end my life. She probably had a lot to tell her friends in the cafeteria the next day.

Eventually, I got to see the psychiatrist, a young woman in ill-fitting jeans and a T-shirt. She seemed distracted and ready to push me on through so she could take the next person and the next, until her day of drudgery ended. She quickly decided I was probably just depressed. I told her about my extensive family history with bipolar disorder, and she abruptly changed her mind. "Well, I guess you're bipolar," she said, smacking her gum. I was stunned by her sudden switch but felt relieved.

Finally, I could exhale. Someone was going to save me.

As I was leaving, she said, "It will be about two weeks before Chris can get you a prescription."

My heart dropped to the center of the earth. "But I want to die and no one is helping me. Please, please, please help me."

"Sorry, he's swamped. There's nothing I can do."

Chris was one door over; I had seen him when he walked by, standing over stacks of files. Couldn't he sign a piece of paper really quickly? It would take seconds. I wasn't asking for any drugs with street value. I didn't want to get high. I just wanted to stay alive.

She walked me back to the waiting area, where I collapsed onto the dirty floor and started begging for my life. "Please help me; I want to die. Save me! Why is no one helping me?"

Her eyes glazed over. She was numb to this.

If I had been bleeding out on the floor that day, someone would have stepped in to rescue me. But my illness was internal, hidden away in the gray matter of my brain, and no one saw it. I was just a number in their system, and no one was willing to cut the red tape to save my life. They sent me home to wait.

I could barely see to drive home. I called Summer, who couldn't understand me through the sobs. I repeated over and over again. "Why won't anyone help me?"

I called Noah, and he rushed to meet me at home. Summer was at work. The two of them started calling psychiatrists around town, trying to advocate for me and find resources. I thrashed around on my bed, going in and out of consciousness. My body was trembling so violently that my teeth were chattering. I was going into shock. About that time, my friend Laura came by to bring me a worship CD. She walked into my room, saw me lying there shaking and helpless, and laid her tiny body right on top of mine. As she prayed for comfort and healing, my body and mind eventually calmed. As soon as they did, I made the decision to admit myself to another hospital since there were no other options available for immediate psychiatric help. Noah had learned of a hospital with an open bed, so I would not need to wait. Even though I had just escaped a place like it, I knew I had to try again to get help. It was unbearable to stay in my present state.

The hospital was closer to my home than the other one, and it was an all-women's unit, which I found comforting. I was terrified that the available bed would be given away and I would be stuck again, so I got in the car without even bringing a toothbrush or clean underwear. I slumped against the car door as Noah drove, and the shaking returned. As we pulled up to the ER, I started freaking out. It hadn't even been one day since I was released from one of these prisons! Despite my terror, I walked in. I signed in, filling in my reason for the visit, "I want to die," and laid my body out on the seats of the waiting room.

The nurses working that morning were incredibly tender. They took me back to a dark, closed-off waiting room. I lay down and covered my face with a cloth. I couldn't bear my sorrow. After I answered pages of questions, they transferred me to an open room without a curtain. I had begged them not to put me anywhere with a curtain because of the traumatic memories of what I had recently experienced. The nurses went out of their way to make sure I felt safe. While I waited to go upstairs to the women's psych unit, Noah played praise music quietly and held my hand. Our pastor called me on the phone, but I don't recall anything he said.

Finally, I was told that a room was ready for me. I was so weak that I could barely stand, so I was placed in a wheelchair. When the door to the psych unit opened, I felt like I was entering heaven. Colored pictures covered the walls, many with affirmations written on them. The one in front of the blood pressure station said, "You are beautiful." A few months earlier I would probably have rolled my eyes at the cheesiness of it all, but now it was like balm to my broken spirit to see that beauty, such a stark contrast from where I had just been. The nurse, who was one of the most nurturing and genuine persons I have ever met, wheeled me down the hall to my room. Along the way, we passed an inviting-looking group room filled with puzzles and books. We came to my room—a room with a door and a beautifully colored sign that said *Helen Joy* with a little flower drawn on the end. I read it again. *Helen Joy.* They saw me. I was real. In the room were a hospital bed, a desk and chair, and a bathroom of my very own. I collapsed on the bed in relief. This was what I had needed all along.

The strip search was incredibly respectful and painless, and afterwards I was allowed to wear my own underwear and clothes. They brought me food that they had been saving for me, and after I ate, a large, graceful nurse tucked me into bed. She touched my shoulder, and she said my name.

PIECE BY PIECE

When my eyes opened the next morning, I felt sick again. Even though I was safe within the walls of the hospital, I was still haunted by memories of the other place. My mind was racing with images, like I was flipping through the pages of a book. I tried to wake myself up from the nightmare, but I was already awake.

I poked my head out of my door and looked down the hallway, curious. I didn't see anyone, so I stepped out in my hospital gown and shuffled towards the group room. My arms were crossed in front of my chest like a shield of protection. I saw other women trickling out of their rooms. Most of them were hardened and frightening, but a few women seemed normal, like me. As I looked around, I silently thanked God that there were no men here. Men with their poisonous thoughts and their desires to rape and destroy.

Before they let us in for breakfast, we gathered around a framed print of the serenity prayer.

God, grant me the serenity to accept the things I cannot   change,
The courage to change the things I can,
And the wisdom to know the difference.

Everyone recited it quickly while I sat wide-eyed and silent. They seated me next to a woman with a pure and innocent round face. She was about thirty years old and was dressed in dull gray sweats. She was so beautiful I couldn't stop glancing sideways at her as I pushed my eggs around. She ate hunched over her plate, using her fingers to force food onto her fork in a childlike manner. Suddenly, the voice of a five-year-old girl started speaking to me: "I want more milk, please." I looked around, confused. Again, a little girl's voice asked for more milk. The question was coming from the woman next to me. A nurse came over and whispered to me that this beautiful woman had dissociative identity disorder, and the child speaking was one of her alternate personalities. I was stunned. I had heard of this in movies, but it had seemed so abstract. By the end of the meal, the woman had returned to her true age and voice.

After we ate, we each wrote down and shared one goal we wanted to achieve that day. For me, it was to talk to the doctor on staff. For two other women, it was simply to shower. Making a small goal every day sustained us in the limbo of getting well. And it showed how life-giving something as simple as a shower can be.

Before everyone had shared their goals, I was called into the doctor's office for my appointment. I was greeted by a grandfatherly man, sharply dressed. He seemed kind and gentle, and I felt comforted by him. But during our chat, I found him to also be dismissive. He didn't ask questions and instead tried to analyze my marital problems and teach me a coping skill to deal with them. I cried a lot, and he seemed to think I was overreacting, which distressed me more. By the end of our session, he told me he didn't think I was bipolar, I was probably "just depressed." I was shocked. I told him, just as I had told my previous therapists, about my father and the many other family members who were bipolar. I told him about being diagnosed by three different experts. But he was set on it. "Bipolar is overdiagnosed. I think a small dose of antidepressant will help you."

I recalled hearing how taking an antidepressant when you had bipolar disorder was a big no-no, so I asked him about that. He casually dismissed my concern. I was exhausted from the fight, so I agreed to the diagnosis. That morning I was given a tiny white pill—a pill that would nearly kill me.

Noah brought me my things: my journal, some clothes, and a book. It felt lovely to have my own belongings with me. I arranged my room. Towel here. Comb there. Three dresses folded neatly away. The control felt wonderful to my brain. It was in stark contrast to how I felt in my six-bedroom house full of things. After my room was set up, I wandered out to the group room to browse through the shelves. In the middle of the many books I found a one-thousand-piece puzzle of a mouse sitting on top of a saxophone. I collected it into my arms and walked quickly by the TV, eyes down. The energy the TV gave off hurt me physically and mentally—panic accompanied by a burning sensation all over my body. Frequently during that week, it felt like my mind would skip, like a scratched CD. My brain gave off visual neon colors that clouded my eyes. I wasn't able to read, and I was barely able to write.

I retreated to the solitude of my room, where I was protected from stimulation. Laying out my puzzle was soothing. Turning over each piece, one by one, felt purposeful. As long as I worked on the puzzle, I could move forward, one piece at a time.

Throughout my stay there, I attended about six classes or groups a day, and afterwards I would hurry back to my puzzle and the safety of my room. As I worked, I heard things happening in the unit. Julia, the woman with the alternate personalities, was screaming and crying in her little-girl voice as they tried to give her a shower. Something horrible must have happened to her in a shower. Nichole, a frequent drug abuser, was cussing at her grandmother on the phone and scratching at her nicotine patch. They had taken her kids away, which I gathered was common for her. Kate was a nurturing grandmother who had been committed by her doctor when she expressed thoughts of suicide. She was angry and desperate to get out to take care of her pregnant daughter and grandchild, but as the days went on she softened and was grateful for the time to heal. Megan was a petite college student who was endearing from the moment I met her. She had been admitted after her boyfriend found cuts up and down her arms. Nancy supposedly had an injured foot that she insisted was in unbearable pain, and no matter which doctors came and told her there was nothing wrong with it, she still demanded narcotics. She also demanded too much macaroni, too much sweet tea, too much of everything. She sat on a chair in the hall like a queen. Nancy had no car, no home, no family.

I listened to the chatter with rapt curiosity but stayed in my room. I didn't want to be a bother. I didn't want to take up space. I melted into the walls and kept my head down.

Hour by hour, piece by piece, the jigsaw puzzle became a picture, and I started feeling a swelling sense of pride. Every time I went to group, I updated the patients on my progress. They didn't care, but I still told them. I called Summer and updated her on my progress too. Even though it felt longer, less than twenty-four hours after starting, I finished it. It felt glorious. I raced into the hall, yelling, "I finished my puzzle!" No one said anything; they weren't the slightest bit distracted from watching TV or sleeping. I called Summer and asked her to update my Facebook status with this: "Just finished a 1,000-piece puzzle. #blessed."

After my puzzle was done, reality started to set in. The unit was full of women who were depressed and slept all day long. I could hear the snores as I walked down the hallway. How could this be? No matter what I did, I couldn't sleep. I was kept alert by the colors in my brain and the images and sound bites that bombarded me. I spent a lot of time pacing the halls and making phone calls to the people whose numbers I had managed to remember. I talked in a hushed voice, standing at the hall phone and picking at the remnants of tape stuck to the wall. It was on one of these calls to the outside that I learned that my friend, whose birth I had promised to attend, had delivered her baby girl. She described a beautiful infant to me that I was left to only imagine. I also found out that Summer landed her dream job. Life was moving on outside, and I was stuck, both physically and mentally.

I kept track of who I had called and timed myself to the very last second to call them back casually, so as not to seem desperate. Every second I waited was excruciating. I called Summer ten times a day— though forty would barely have felt like enough. Loneliness flooded my bones, and even though this place was heaven compared to the other, I wanted out. I wanted to be normal again, to be with my family, to play with my children. Thanksgiving was just a few days away, and I was determined to leave before then. After all, I was "just depressed." I should be able to normalize quickly at home now that I was medicated.

Every few days they had one and a half hours set aside for visitors that we had preapproved. Many women refused to see their visitors for safety reasons or simply because they didn't want to wake up. Sometimes they showed up anyways, and were escorted off of the floor. My pastor came one day and sat across the room from me on my chair while I sat on my bed, cross-legged. He looked into my eyes and said, "If you had died, Helen Joy, it would have crushed our church in a way we would never recover from. I probably would have quit the ministry." His eyes were sincere and full of promise. It was the first time someone had understood how near death I was.

My four sisters came in after him and gently laid me down on the bed, running their fingers through my hair and down my back. We barely spoke. Their faces were contorted in hurt and confusion, but they just loved me the best way they knew how. It was exactly what I needed. I let Noah come at the end of my stay, but only for a few minutes. Something about him triggered feelings that were dark and scary, but he held me and stayed quiet.

After visitation, Beth, the activities director who was a retired chaplain, started a group session. First, we had to play our feelings on a bongo drum. After hearing the erratic patterns of the women before me, I lay my hand on the white, stretched drum and played nothing before passing it on. Then animal pictures were pinned to our backs, and we asked each other yes or no questions, trying to determine what animal we each had. I asked for the hardest one, since I like a challenge. After quite some time I managed to guess that it was an octopus, and everyone celebrated and congratulated me as though I had just finished a triathlon. Apparently, I was the first person ever to guess that one.

I walked back to my room with a smile on my face, giggling at how funny it felt to feel joy from such a small success. That game shattered the walls I had put up. Soon after, I came out of my room and chatted with the other patients and felt my old self coming back. The pill was already doing its job.

I started getting to know Julia. I was attracted to her. Surrounded by women who were hard and rugged, with missing teeth, she was bright, young, and healthy looking. I loved watching her laugh, hoping I could laugh again one day soon. In those short days we became friends. She would scribble in an old, worn composition notebook during every group, and I would glance over, curious about her markedly different handwriting styles, wishing I could read it.

One evening after dinner Julia took me into the common room and brought her notebook and her blanket to cuddle up next to me. She opened it to show me. There was children's scratch, spelling out just a few simple words—piercing words of being hurt and scared. There was the terrible handwriting of a teenage boy writing angry, hateful things. There was an abusive whore who destroyed her body. There was a kind woman, probably the mother she wished she had. Piece by piece her story came together.

Her first memory was being raped with candlesticks by her mother when she was just a baby in diapers. This violation occurred again and again, to prepare her for being sold for sex. At five years old, she was paraded through an oceanside Miami mansion with a dozen other little girls, all wearing sheer, white nightgowns. There, her false virginity was auctioned off, and her innocence was destroyed by an old white man. The next morning she tried to sit through her first day of kindergarten, bleeding and confused. When the teacher asked her what her name was, she couldn't remember. This was the first self-preserving split that occurred inside her. There were many women in the psych unit from whom I would not have believed this story, but I believed Julia. Her earnest face lit up as she searched my eyes for understanding and belief. She saw my compassion and continued to share her story and her alternate personalities.

She was caught and abused in a satanic cult her mother was a member of. Nearly every evening she was forced, naked, into a room with one-way glass, on display and up for bid for the night. She slept only a few hours each night and struggled to stay awake at school. I don't understand why a teacher didn't see her, help her. How did she get overlooked? This happened for years and years before she escaped.

Several times, when Julia was her five-year-old self, she would talk about her little brother with me. One night I asked her about him, and her eyes grew wide, wondering how I knew about him. "No one knows about him," she whispered. I sat in silence, waiting as she gathered her thoughts. After a few minutes, she tearfully whispered to me that when he was a baby, her mother offered him as a sacrifice, and he was shot inside of a white plastic cooler. The cult members filled a chalice with his blood and forced the girls to drink. They weren't allowed to cry or they, too, would be killed. Julia's face grew white and filled with horror as she told me. I believed her. The evil was so thick that it made me gag.

Julia finally escaped as a young teen and spent years on the streets, sleeping with drug dealers to keep herself in a state where she didn't ever have to be in her right body or mind. One day she managed to claw her way out, but her mind was left shattered into a million pieces. I don't know why she trusted me that night. Sometimes I wish she hadn't. I can't unknow the things she told me. I still think of her often, her joyful face that shone through her darkness, and I hope that she's safe.

When the doctors finally decided I could be released the day before Thanksgiving, I started pacing the halls, willing the time to pass. My puzzle was back on its shelf, and I was aching for home. Julia came into the hallway holding a small, foam ball that had been left behind by one of the group leaders. We started tossing it back and forth down the hallway. We were joined by two other women, and we all sat on the floor rolling the ball between our legs, laughing the most pure and delightful belly laughs. Our bodies had nearly forgotten how. We did this for more than an hour, and I don't think that unit had ever heard such laughter as it did that afternoon. It was the best medicine we received there. Four broken women in a moment of relief from their pain. A lifting of their burdens, if just for an hour. Real joy pouring from their mouths as they threw their heads back like children.

THANKSGIVING

When I stepped out of the psych unit to go home, I felt a little bit of hope bubble up in my heart. Maybe life could be different. Maybe I could shake this horrible season of being locked up. I also felt a bit of shame as I returned to the family I had abandoned again and the people who had to carry them while I was gone. As soon as I walked into the door of our home, the kids all came to hug me. I braced for their hurt or their anger, but instead they again asked cheerfully, "How was your trip, Mama?"

The house was familiar, but also foreign. The comfort of it wrapped me like a blanket, yet the things around me felt strange. Shelves full of books, closets full of clothes, cabinets full of food, all available whenever I wanted them. Strewn around my house were signs of people loving us. Word had spread about our situation, and our counters and tables were covered with cards, stacked and cleaned Tupperware from meals brought over, and small tokens of thoughtfulness. I found out that one of my girlfriends had made three sets of lunches and dropped them at our door so Noah didn't have to worry about making them for the kids. I heard about the army of people who weaved in and out, watching the kids, doing our laundry, and praying. It felt unreal to be loved like that. No one asked; they just came.

It was Thanksgiving morning, and Noah woke me up early and told me to come outside. I wrapped myself in a blanket with bleary eyes and matted hair, took my small white pill, and went downstairs. Out the window I saw runners jogging by and a chair waiting for me on our lawn. It was the yearly Turkey Trot, and I sat and watched as our town ran through our front road. One by one, people would cut out of the race, run up to me, and give me a hug. "I'm glad you're here." "Seeing your face is the best part of my day." "I'm the most grateful for you this Thanksgiving." People plopped these offerings into my lap. Sorrow, mixed with gratefulness, overflowed on that chilly Thanksgiving morning.

After all the racers had run by, we headed to my mother's for Thanksgiving lunch. I felt fragile, but I smiled and gave hugs all around. I could tell everyone was holding their breath as they watched how I would behave. I thought of the women still in the psych unit, eating off of their dull, brown trays. I felt sad and guilty for being free. I wanted to tell everyone about Julia, but every time I brought it up, most people would switch subjects. No one wanted to think of things like that. That afternoon, we played our annual tennis tournament. I was wearing a long dress, but I borrowed my sister's tennis shoes. The sun warmed my skin, and I felt alive for the first time in months. They could have been burying me today. I knew that. They knew that. We didn't say it, but we knew it. It was a Thanksgiving day for sure.

DROWNING IN AIR

In the weeks that followed, I took my pill faithfully every day, hoping it would continue to make me feel better. I believed it was working, but still I felt hollow inside. Not dark anymore, just hollow. Sometimes I wondered if I was real.

Since my release from the hospital, I had mostly kept to myself, with the exception of a few close friends popping in here and there. I wanted to rejoin society and attend all the holiday parties going on, but I felt paralyzed. One early December day I thought that maybe I could attend the fortieth birthday party of a friend that was planned for that evening. No one expected me to go, but I decided that it would be my rejoining day. But by the time Noah and I were ready to leave, I had second thoughts. I don't know if it was the idea of being surrounded by people, some of whom I didn't know, or having to inanely chat about holiday plans or the niceties of middle-class life when I had just survived hell on earth, but the thought of it all started to close in on me. I didn't want to go, yet I felt like I needed to. I voiced my fears, and Noah assured me that we could leave anytime I wanted, all I had to do was whisper the word. As we left, I adjusted my dress in the mirror and stuffed down all the bad memories. I would be normal. I would be fun.

Bravely walking into the small, cramped room of our friend's home, I nervously glanced around. Some eyes looked at me with tenderness and some didn't even know who I was. It was like I was carrying a secret, and it reminded me of those first days of finding out I was pregnant when no one knew. Except that this secret was nasty and ugly. The bustle of chattering adults, the lights, and the clinking of ice in the holiday cocktails filled my ears and lulled me into a twilight zone feeling. I laughed, I hugged, and I managed to be a real and normal person that night. Noah was having a wonderful time; it was like he was shedding a month's worth of worry, and his booming laugh echoed more and more with each old-fashioned he downed. As people started leaving, I whispered to Noah that I wanted to go home. He shrugged me off. Again and again I begged to leave, but he was enjoying being charming and carefree for the first time in weeks. I finally grabbed his hand, dragged him to our car, and hopped in the driver's seat. At home, instead of him putting me to bed, snug and safe, like he had since I came home from the hospital, I put him to bed in his clothes with his shoes still on. He was snoring when his head hit the pillow.

As I got myself ready for bed, my mind started flipping through memories of the previous few weeks, with the images and sound bites coming faster and faster. The smacking of those men in the circle outside my room grew to a deafening roar. Then I heard an audible crack—and that is when I saw my first hallucination.

I walked out of our room to get something in the hall, and I ran into my own feet with my shoulder. They were wearing worn, mismatched socks, with a hole in the left toe. I slowly turned my gaze upwards and saw my entire body hanging from the ceiling. I could make out every detail of my form. My dark and twisted face stared down hauntingly at me. Instead of being terrified, I ran to my computer and searched the internet for instructions on how to hang oneself. Images, chat rooms, and step-by-step guides filled my screen. My heart was pounding, and the thrill of doing something like that, so final, so violent, pulsed through my body. Hours passed, and as I wandered through the house, I started seeing my body hanging everywhere—in my bedroom, in the hallway, all the way down our stairway to the foyer. Clones. An army of the dead. I walked through them, pushing each one out of the way so I could pass through like I was navigating an eerie corn maze. The weight of the bodies nearly knocked me down as they swung back and forth.

I tried to wake Noah. I shook him; I screamed at him. He didn't respond. I started to feel like the bodies were going to bury me alive. I lay next to Noah, sobbing and looking at mindless things on Facebook, trying to erase the searing images of my hanging corpses. Suddenly, I could not inhale. I couldn't catch a breath. I gasped for Noah to call 911. I yelled that I was dying. He continued snoring. I called Summer, who miraculously hadn't put her phone on silent that night.

I . . . can't . . . breathe," I said, panting between words.

"I. . . am . . . dying."

Summer stayed on the phone with me, instructing me to inhale and exhale as she drove the one mile to my home. When she arrived, I was lying in my driveway in my nightgown, my face on the cold asphalt. I had just experienced my first hallucination and my first panic attack. This was my first time drowning in clean, fresh air. Summer drove me to her home and put me in her guest bed, lying next to me just like the

Native American woman I had envisioned in the hospital. Eyes locked with mine, she told me to breathe, and she told me I was safe. The crack that I heard that night was the start of my mind being split open—and it was all because of a little pill I wasn't supposed to be taking in the first place.

DROPS OF LOVE

I think previously I would frantically collect drops of love—

Clutch them close until they evaporated.

Now it is raining love, and every drop is slipping through my fingers.

YOU CAN'T PRAY AWAY
MENTAL ILLNESS

One cold weekend morning I woke up and I announced that I wanted to get a Christmas tree. Noah was surprised, since I was still recovering, still weak and traumatized. But I was determined, so we loaded the kids into our van and drove an hour or so through the winding mountains to a large tree farm on the side of a hill. I flinched at every red brake light, gripping Noah's hand in fear. My nerves were raw, and it felt like I had new, fresh skin that had never been touched by air. We trudged through the rows of trees, weaving in and out of happy families laughing. Then I saw it—a tree on the hill, reaching to the light. *That's me,* I thought. *I'm on a hill, and I have to reach harder than others to find the sunlight.* I was there reaching; it was there reaching.

"I want that one," I whispered.

During my long days in the hospitals, I had lain in bed dreaming of a Christmas tree by the fire. I was sure the magic would seal up the wounds in our family and we could begin again. I could begin again.

That night, when my tree was standing in our living room, I made hot cocoa, crying when I spilled it on the floor. We tried to decorate, and I ended up screaming and lashing out. Noah got me a blanket and

I curled up on the couch, protecting the ones I loved from myself. I watched them hang each precious ornament on the branches, the ornaments lumpy and off center. I watched them laugh and sing, and I felt so far away. I felt like I wasn't really there, like I wasn't even real.

That first part of December was a mix of beauty and pain. I was always stretching like that tree on the hill, reaching for hope and joy. My first appointment with the best psychiatrist in town (thanks to a friend who called in a favor for me) was scheduled for two weeks from when I had been released—a distant finish line that I counted down to every day. *Eight more days. Seven more days. Six more days.* Those days were long, and the nights were longer. In the daytime I managed to bake cookies, watch the Christmas parade, and shop for presents, but the darkness brought me back to the battlefront every night. While my family slept, I experienced hours of visions, impulses to hurt myself, and panic attacks. Thoughts of suicide became a constant ringing in my ears.

Some mornings I couldn't stand to be alone, and I would beg Noah to stay with me. Sometimes he did; sometimes he took me to my mom. She bathed me and fed me, brushing my hair. She would tell me to think good thoughts, and she would pray over me. I felt rotten inside as I tried to be cheerful.

Word once again spread about my ordeal, and love was bountifully poured onto me and my family. Letters and packages littered my doorstep; texts and calls flowed like a river throughout my days. The words sent to me were beautiful, powerful. Under other circumstances they would have been life-giving, but I felt nothing but emptiness. I heard the words, but I couldn't grab on. The love was slipping through my fingers. Not a thing anyone said or did could save me.

I went to two different therapists during the week. I lay in my bed with my hand on my heart, listening to the words of worship songs, aching for relief. I sat outside in the winter sun; I took my little white pill. I was doing everything I had been told to do to heal.

When things weren't getting better, I overheard the word *demons* getting tossed around by family members and people in church. Was I possessed by demons? Did my house have demons in it, and was that why my depression started when we moved? My desperate mind latched onto the idea, and I became fixated on making it right. I went to my pastor, who told me that I couldn't be possessed by a demon because I had Christ inside of me. He said it so gently and clearly, there wasn't a single doubt in his mind.

I reached out to my precious friend Laura, who had just attended a seminar on healing prayer. Throughout my life, I cringed when people prayed strongly around me. The moans and groans and the breathiness kept my eyes opened wide in discomfort instead of closed in reverence. This reaction came from watching my mother, my church, and camp. From flashing back to praying for my dad in the hospital or praying to keep a pregnancy, prayer didn't work. It felt foolish to me, and I never felt heard.

Laura was opposite of the loud, pushy women I had interacted with over my lifetime. She was gentle and earnest. Her cold hands held mine, and her eyes brimmed with tears as she told me truths about God and truths about me. I trusted her, so I went to her church and joined her in a small room with two other women. As I sat there, I noticed holes in the sweater I had worn for the past three months. Ragged, like me. My hair was tangled. Desperation clung to my heart. But these women didn't seem to care. They were real and unrefined in their manner. They were gentle. They didn't have to carry on in a dramatic fashion for God to hear them; in fact, they whispered one sentence, and that was enough. I felt honored to hear them call out to God on my behalf. At one point, one woman quietly said, "Jesus, close the door to suicide in Helen Joy's life." That was it. No wailing, moaning, or grunting. Simple. Expectant. I left feeling cared for, but the darkness was still there, around me like a shroud. I wasn't surprised that God didn't hear me. Maybe He wasn't even there.

The women prayed with me a few more times. They came over to my house one morning, sat around my living room, and sprinkled their prayers in the air like holy water. I wanted it to work. I wanted the oppression to lift and for me to be rescued from the quicksand. I wanted to rejoin reality. I wanted to feel my family's love. But when they left, I was still the same and hopelessness filled the air around me.

In reality, the chemicals in my brain were misfiring, but it was easier for people to blame it on demons. It became easier for me to condemn myself for my lack of faith than to admit that something was out of my control. I was trying so hard. My journals were scrawled with a determination to be better, and at the same time I sank deeper and deeper into darkness.

You can't pray away mental illness. You can't always take away scary thoughts by reading the Bible. Sometimes, maybe, but my prayers and the prayers of those women did not heal me when we asked. My brain was tortured by chemicals, not by demons.

On the morning of December 6, I awoke to a text that my mama-client had finally gone into labor. I was so relieved. The terrors of the previous night faded, and I felt ready to do something I was good at. As I walked up to the hospital, I glanced at the window that had been mine just two weeks before. I entered bravely. All day I supported my new mama: massaging, encouraging, photographing. I did well. She did well. I was able to work like I always did. It made me feel like I wasn't broken after all. But when the baby was born, I didn't cry like I usually did. I felt joy that she was here, but I also felt like I was watching the birth from behind that thick piece of glass I knew so well. I was tired, I told myself. If I slept, I would feel better. I left young mama and daddy all snuggled up with promises to return in the morning to check in. I crashed into sleep at home without sensing the darkness and I thought that maybe, like that new babe, I had finally come out into the light on the other side.

FUNERAL

I can see my funeral. I can feel the sun. I can feel the sharp wind. I can smell the dirt being unearthed.

No one is crying. It is still.

My poor children, my numb, confused children, look over the deep hole, wondering where Mama has gone. Heartbroken, I try to come back to them. It's too late. It's too late.

If you could kill yourself by simply willing yourself not to breathe, I would have been long gone from this earth.

PSYCHOSIS

The details of this night are jagged, horrific, grim, and I want to hide them away in the darkness where they belong. But bringing them into the light of the world has eased the shame I feel. The light exposes these memories and takes their power away.

The day after I attend a birth is always hard for me. The high wears off, and I am always a little bit sad. Exhaustion, melancholy, and reverence weigh heavily on me. And the awe that the miracle of birth inspires in me, which never gets old, makes me feel oddly detached from the world around me because I'm still reeling from the magic while everyone else is trudging through their normal day.

It was dark and cloudy that first day after the birth. I slept a little, went to check on my clients, and returned home in a fog. That afternoon, my dear friend Rebekah drove two hours to see me for the first time since my unraveling began. She hugged me so tightly it felt like it was the last hug we would ever have. We climbed into my bed, piled high with quilts, and just lay there, grateful that I had made it through. I told her about the terrifying stuff and about being so lonely. She listened and played with my hair. She left as night began to fall, and the familiar dread of the darkness and the chilling loneliness started creeping in once more.

Feeling connected with my children had become increasingly difficult. It was like I was underwater—everything was muffled and slow. That morning I had made one goal for the whole day: to snuggle up and watch Elf as a family. I was fixated on making it happen. A friend had dropped off a crockpot full of dinner. It was beef, which I don't eat, so I grabbed a yogurt and took it upstairs to eat by myself, away from the noise and the little faces I felt so distant from. Noah invited a friend over to share the meal, and our house was filled with laughter and chatter as everyone ate downstairs. I started feeling strong surges inside my body. I was wringing my hands and tapping my feet back and forth, willing the minutes to go by. I wondered if my blood sugar was low since I had replaced a proper dinner with a small yogurt.

We need to watch the movie! We need to watch the movie! I chanted to myself. I held onto my only goal for the day like a lifeline.

I looked around my room frantically, anxious for relief. I saw my Bible and opened it up, reading furiously. I was flipping through pages at an alarming rate, whispering "Jesus Christ, Jesus Christ," over and over again, trying to push away the darkness overtaking me. I continued reading and chanting until the kids bounded up to my bed for the movie. All at once, the chaos inside was matched by the chaos outside, and I felt tossed about like a ship in a hurricane. Noah brought the downstairs TV up to our bedroom and started setting it up. Rolling over onto my stomach, I desperately started browsing Instagram on my phone, trying to drown everything out, to detach. Click by click, I sank deeper—babies, makeup, memes, cutting. I stumbled onto the account of a teenage girl who uploaded videos and pictures of herself cutting her arms, poems about suicide, and pain-stained captions. I watched the videos hunched over my screen as my children playfully jumped around me and my husband fiddled with the TV. When the movie finally started, the goal of my entire day, I couldn't even pay attention. I was hooked on a part of Instagram I had never seen before. Darkness, shock, similarities to what obsessive thoughts were plaguing me. I would fake a laugh at a funny part of the movie, but mostly my eyes were on my phone. No one noticed I wasn't watching.

Before I knew it, the movie had ended and Noah took them all to bed. I went back to browsing babies and makeup, my heart still pounding. After everyone had finally fallen asleep, Noah came to bed and flopped down next to me. I lay there, eyes wide open, as energy pulsed through me. Without warning, I slipped out of my body and flew to the ceiling, looking down on my bed from above. I saw myself sprawled out, tangled in my quilt, and stared into my own terrified eyes. My mind filled with visions of me killing myself—much like that night I saw my body hanging everywhere, but a hundred times faster. Over and over, I saw myself running to our stairwell and throwing myself over, head first. I heard my bones break, and I looked down at my mangled body. I saw myself run to the bathroom, smash my head into my mirror and take a shard of glass to slice open my throat. I watched myself bleed out, like I was watching a movie. I started voicing these visions to Noah in hopes that he would stop me from going through with it.

"Guard the bathroom, I'm gonna slit my throat."

"Guard the stairs, I want to jump. I want to hear my bones break."

The visions came faster and faster. So fast I couldn't repeat what I saw out loud anymore. I was speaking so fast, it was barely understandable. The shadow was thick, and my visions were vibrant. Noah texted four friends to ask for prayer, and the next thing I knew, Summer was at my side. I continued spewing out the violent hallucinations in my head. Looking down from above, I could see inside of myself, and there was an enormous, grotesque, beating heart where my stomach should be. "Please, cut this heart out of me!" I begged. Noah ran outside and called the mobile crisis response system for help. A few minutes later, a kind-looking man entered my bedroom and sat next to me, asking questions. I described everything—the belly-heart, the suicides, the darkness, the cutting I watched on Instagram. Over and over my visions cycled. Bones crushing, throat bleeding, heart beating. I tried to force myself to think of things that were mild and safe. I thought about the box of popsicles in our freezer, then saw myself melting them and shoving them down my throat until I couldn't breathe. Soft blankets became nooses, spoons were shoved into my arms and legs, severing my arteries.

My long-awaited psychiatrist appointment, when I finally was to get the prescription I so desperately needed, was the next morning at ten o'clock. That appointment had been my goal for the last two weeks. Everyone was determined to get me stable enough to go and avoid another hospital stay. Everyone was up for the challenge of keeping me alive until then.

I was so obsessed with throwing myself down the stairs that Noah, Summer, and the mobile crisis man decided to take me. They heaved me up out of bed and surrounded me as I walked down the stairs. I wanted to jump so badly that my body burned. Part of me was grinning, thinking about it; the other part was terrified that I would do it. When we got downstairs, a tidal wave of new ways to hurt myself crashed over me. The pulsing and beating inside grew warm and sickly. An irresistible force led me to the kitchen where I tried to open our knife drawer. Someone stopped me and led me to the couch while the others hid dangerous objects from around the house. Summer sat next to me, rubbing my back, as I chanted out new ways I was scared I would kill myself. The pressure to act was so great that in one second I knew I could bypass her and do the things I saw played out in my mind. As I sat there, belly-heart still beating, I had a time-lapse vision of the creation of an ice cream scoop built out of small daggers. It looked medieval and heavy. I was drawn to it. I described it to Summer and begged her to make one so I could scoop the heart from my belly like soft ice cream. "Please, please, please make it for me." I said breathlessly.

That was abruptly overtaken by a vision of myself throwing my children out the window from the third floor of our house, with the excruciating aftermath. I closed my eyes and tried to will away the movie I was seeing, but it kept playing, over and over again, forcing me to watch myself do the unspeakable. I said out loud what I was driven to do, what I was terrified I would do. Summer went to tell the Noah and the man from mobile crisis. As soon as she left me to talk to Noah and the man from mobile crisis, I looked at my hands and watched them transform into red claws. I could see every bump and crack; they smelled like ashes. Whispers from the other room surrounded me as I tried to erase the images from my head. Shaking the violent pictures out of my head, pulling at my hair, and digging my nails into my skin, I called for Summer to show her my claws. She didn't see them.

Someone gave me Tylenol PM and melatonin. "I think this is caused by the antidepressant she's taking," I heard the mobile crisis man say as my head started swirling with the hope of a brief coma.

Their goal was to get me into a deep sleep so I could make it till my morning appointment. They lay me down on the couch and covered my twitching body with a blanket. I'm not sure if it took hours or minutes, but the visions finally faded away, and I fell into a restless sleep.

That night, doctors say, my brain created a thousand neural pathways, bursting, crackling, sparking until they burst into flames. That night, I was marked with permanent, invisible scars that I will carry the rest of my life.

COCAINE YOGURT

I woke up suddenly, eyes popping open. I was still lying on the green couch in my living room, the visions of the night before still vibrant and incessant. Terror flooded me. "Noah! Noah! Noah! Help me!" He rushed to my side, having just gotten the kids out the door for school. He knelt next to me and looked deep into my eyes; I saw such heartache and fear in his, like he wasn't seeing me but a terrifying creature instead.

It was the morning of my first psychiatric appointment; just three more hours to wait. I had almost made it. But my mind started revving up, the malicious thoughts coming faster and faster like an avalanche down a mountain. Noah got me up the stairs and to bed safely, which wasn't easy. The journey to the bedroom was horrifying; I was bombarded with images of myself and my children at the bottom of the stairs, twisted and broken in a pile. No matter how much I tried to shut out the ugly thoughts and visions, they shoved their way back. Once in bed, I lay quiet for a few minutes, and Noah started getting ready for work. But my uncontrollable outbursts resumed.

"Lock the door!"

"I want to jump!"

"Guard the mirror, I want to cut."

"Don't let me eat the plants."

"Don't let me jam a toothbrush down my throat."

"Don't let me hang myself with your belt."

"I'm gonna run. I'm gonna jump."

"Guard the windows!"

Noah called my friend Amy and asked her to bring me a bagel for breakfast and sit with me so he could have one meeting before my appointment. Amy had become a kindred spirit over the course of a year of meeting together. I took photos for her, and she helped me get my shit together. She had spent many hours talking me out of shame and guilt. She lifted up the good parts of me and helped with the parts that needed helping. She was my life doula. She walked in, bagel in hand, bold but calm. Within the first seconds of her being in the room, I started spouting off the visions flipping through my head and the impulses I felt could be executed in seconds.

She didn't even wait a minute. "Your brain is on fire, and we need to go back to the hospital," she said matter-of-factly.

But I was so close to the appointment! I said I would try harder, I would find a way to quiet it all.

"I don't feel like I can keep you safe. We have to go," she said.

"I'll go if I can bring a new puzzle and some slippers."

"Deal."

Even though I had been to the hospital twice and knew how important it was to have my own things with me, I couldn't pack a bag. I felt like I could move faster than light and there were too many dangers. Amy asked another friend to round up size eight slippers and a puzzle and meet us at admissions.

I adore Amy, and being with her that morning felt like a little bit of fun but in a perverse way. I would tell her I wanted to hear my bones break, then roar with laughter. I knew I was acting like a lunatic, but I couldn't stop. I couldn't wipe the smile off my face, even though I was afraid. Getting downstairs safely was hard. I kept trying to run back, laughing. My fingernails started to itch, and the energy in my arms was surging so powerfully I felt like they were separating from my body. I wrapped them around each other and held them close to my body, like a makeshift straightjacket. I rocked back and forth, back and forth.

"Your brain is on fire," Amy said, as if she were describing the color of my socks.

"I ate a yogurt last night. It had cocaine in it. That's all that's happening here."

In my mind, I could see the thin aluminum top of the yogurt still in my trash can. It had a small hole in it, where someone had injected it with drugs. It was real. I was sure I had been drugged.

During the drive to the hospital, I alternated between trying to jump out of the car, trying to pull my nails off, wrapping my arms around each other, and texting and making phone calls to dozens of people. I even tried calling a friend in Africa before Amy realized what I was doing and took my phone away.

We pulled up to the hospital. My body was pulsing, my fingers were itching, and my arms were burning. I didn't want to go in. I stood there in the cold, looking up at the window that was my room the last time I was there. I had stood at that window looking out to where I was standing right now, willing myself to escape. And here I was, on the other side, going back in. I looked to my right, to the window of the birthing room I had walked out of just a day before. It didn't make sense. Why was I there?

Amy's promise of slippers and a new puzzle woke me out of my haze, and I walked through the sliding door to turn myself over yet again.

The waiting room was empty. My eyes darted around. Dangers, what were the dangers? I was flooded with new visions: impaling myself with a chair leg, drinking the bottle of hand sanitizer. I kept my arms tightly wound around myself. It felt like there were worms crawling under my nails. I tried to scratch them free; I tried to use my teeth to drag them out. My fingers were red and raw, but still I felt the worms. I got to the front desk and looked at the clipboard where I was to write my name, date of birth, and why I was there.

"Helen Joy George," I wrote. "10/12/1985. I am crazy."

Amy scratched out the last part and wrote, "Suicidal ideations and hallucinations."

I was babbling and rocking, so they got me right into triage. I told the nurse about the worms under my nails. She asked me for a urine sample, and I matter-of-factly explained that there would be cocaine in it. Then I asked if she thought I was just high on cocaine. I rattled off a list of reasons I might be there: the cocaine, the worms, the drugs, low blood sugar. I just wanted to be fixed and sent home.

Once in my cubicle in the ER, I spent my time yelling out dangers that needed to be removed and laughing so hard I was crying. Amy smiled warmly at me and at the same time took me seriously. Everyone thought she was my mom. After a little while she needed to pee, and I heard her tell the nurse, "I know she's laughing and she looks like she's okay, but she is not okay." He understood and had all of the equipment moved out of my room—everything but the plastic gloves, which haunted me with their powers of suffocation. When they brought me food, I insisted on eating it with my hands because I could see myself jamming the plastic utensils into my heart or through my carotid artery.

A pretty nurse came to draw my blood. As she was doing it, I saw a tiny man rushing through the veins in my arms. He popped out through the needle and into the vial. He was dressed in purple, with a small hat, and he had a black mustache. His terrified face was pressed against the tube, begging me to save his life.

"There's a small man in there! Let him out!" I yelled.

They showed me the vial. I held it in my hands and swished the red blood around, searching for him. But he was gone.

They were anxious to get me out of the ER and into a place that was safe and secure. A wheelchair was swiftly brought to take me upstairs to the women's unit. Right when I was climbing into the wheelchair, lamenting the fact that my slippers and puzzle hadn't gotten there in time, my beautiful friend Cara showed up. She took my shoes off, placed the slippers on my feet, and loaded the puzzle into my lap. She looked so sad. It reminded me that maybe my family was sad too. My heart sank. The banter and laughter with Amy was fading now, and I had to go to the place where I was alone. This was real.

Once in the women's unit, I was greeted warmly by the staff, who remembered me from two weeks before.

"Please! Can you remove my fingernails? I have worms under them!" I begged the admitting nurse. She gently smiled but ignored my request. They strip-searched me and gave me the welcome folder with no explanation of how things worked. But I knew, and they knew I knew. As soon as they left me there, I saw the shower curtain. It was hung with Velcro strips so that patients could not hang themselves on it, but it seemed the perfect object to suffocate my body with. I ripped it out and threw it in the hall. I also threw my pen, toothbrush, toothpaste, shampoo and conditioner, and comb outside my door. I could see my comb digging into my wrist, my veins threading around it like spaghetti on a fork. Dangers. I bit all my nails to the quick and swallowed them whole so that I couldn't slit my wrists with them. I paced the halls with my arms wound tight until a nurse gave me an injection, which calmed me down. I don't remember the rest of the day.

CRAYONS AND WORMS

I woke up in darkness. A faint glow from under the door was all that illuminated the room. I looked over to the large desk that sat in my room and saw an orange that I had been given to hold the day before, to calm myself down, to ground me. I crept out of bed and held it in my hands. Once frozen, it was now soft and squishy. I dug my fingers into the skin, cracking it open, then set it back down and placed my hands on the surface of the desk, six inches from the orange. White worms crawled out of my fingernails, across the desk, and into the fruit. Dozens, hundreds, thousands. I watched in disbelief. I could hear their bodies scraping against the fake wood of the desk. When the orange was engulfed by wriggling, white bodies, I saw a bottle of olive oil set to the side. I hadn't noticed it before, and the fact that it was glass and in my room seemed absurd. I grabbed it and poured layers and layers of the thick yellow oil onto the orange, drowning every last worm. My fingernails finally stopped itching.

It was four thirty in the morning. I snuck into the hall and asked to use the phone. I had to tell my sister. I was positive there were worms under the fingernails of all my children, and olive oil could be the cure. But I wasn't allowed make a call until eight o'clock. I went back to my room and tried to go back to sleep. My body felt like it had been

194 • Helen Joy George

beaten badly, and the wheel in my head was starting to spin again. I was saturated with new and old thoughts and started writing them down on the back of my welcome folder in illegible scribbles. The more I wrote, the more things popped into my head. I looked around my room and saw my new puzzle. I didn't trust myself to open it. What if I ate all the pieces and choked? What if there was a pod full of gel that I could just hibernate in until my brain was fixed?

Breakfast finally came. I ate with my hands again, my feet and knees bouncing below the table. As I waited to be the first person on the phone, I paced in front of the group room. Glancing in, I saw a bucket of crayons sitting on the table. I knew I would eat them. I called my sister in California. It was five o'clock her time.

"Georgia, can you look up what happens if you swallow fifty crayons?" I whispered into the phone.

She was discombobulated, still half asleep. I could hear her rustling around in bed. "Honey, can you Google 'what happens if you eat fifty crayons?'" she asked her husband.

Silence. Then, "It's not good, HJ."

I told her I didn't feel safe. I didn't know if I could stop myself from ending it all by eating fistfuls of broken crayons from the group room.

I hung up and made another call to Julianna. Before she could pick up, I saw the nurse behind the glass answer the nurses phone and nod, looking at me. "Don't you worry, we won't let her eat any."

Julianna answered and I frantically described in detail the mass exodus of worms from my fingers. I instructed her, step by step, how to remove worms from my three children. Maybe this was why they were always so agitated and squirmy. Yes, surely that was it.

"You promise you'll do it? Do Sullivan's lips too!" I pleaded. I wouldn't hang up until I had a promise.

I was the first person to see the doctor that morning. I walked into his tiny, cluttered office, shaking, rocking from side to side, mind exploding with thoughts, arms wrapped around my body. I sat down and immediately he said in a singsongy voice, "Well, I guess you really are bipolar," like this was a game. He explained that people with bipolar disorder have this kind of reaction to antidepressants. I tried to tell him how scary it had been, tried to remind him that I had asked not to take them. I related the visions, the broken body parts, the dead children. If he felt any guilt at all, he didn't show it. I was to start taking a mood stabilizer—which is what I should have been given weeks before instead of now having to take heavy doses of antipsychotics. The gravity of the situation was just swept under the rug. I left feeling unheard and unseen.

There was something comforting about being on that unit again. I knew the routine. I knew the rules. I knew how to order double portions of mac and cheese for dinner and the codes for using the phones. Despite the familiarity, the people from my last stay were long gone, and there was an emptiness. Gone was Julia and her bright face, gone was the game of catch in the hallway. This time around there were a lot of drug addicts with missing teeth, who slept all day long. There was a childlike woman who had to have a nurse with her every second. Whenever the nurse would glance away, the woman would jump up and bang her head against the wall until she bled all over her cat sweater. She ended up having to wear a helmet.

Then there was Mary, whose situation truly scared me. She was a woman in her nineties who had suffered with bipolar disorder her whole life. She was just waking up from a mixed episode and didn't even know who had been elected as president three weeks before. We were quietly eating lunch one day when someone mentioned Trump, and she nearly choked on her green beans. "You've got to be kidding me! They elected *him*?" We all died laughing. I would watch her from afar, her gummy mouth quivering. Her mind was reeling like mine was, yet her body was wheelchair bound. It never ends, I thought to myself.

In sixty years, will I be spending my holiday season locked up and afraid? As my body disintegrates, will my mind keep up this frantic pace?

When I woke up the second morning of my stay, most of my dark thoughts were gone. Just a few interjected here and there, like static on a radio. I stood at the window and watched the sun come up. The rays streamed into my room. I touched the palm of my hand to the cool glass and whispered, "This battle has been won." I had fought, and I had lived.

Suppressing my mania with heavy sedatives created waves inside of me. I wrote in my journal:

The waves in my body are unbelievably strong. I go from 1000 things to say to blank. My body feels abused and beaten, my mind longs for wholeness.

I got to the point where I felt safe having my comb and toothbrush in my room. I opened my puzzle and finished a thousand pieces in less than a day. I paced, I wrote. I lay in bed, drool pooling in the corners of my mouth.

When Noah came to see me during visiting hours, I couldn't even sit up. This dance between feeling on fire and corpse-like continued throughout four lonely days. Once again I sat alone in my hospital room while my friends frolicked at Christmas parties. I walked the empty halls while my children made cookies.

During our movement group, the volunteer gathered all the women, glassy-eyed and depressed, into the hall for gentle dancing. The volunteer pushed play on the small CD player, and "It's the Most Wonderful Time of the Year" started wafting through the air. Before I knew it, all the women were doing the cancan. Legs kicking side to side, all mixed up. Their toothless grins were bright, their cat pajamas were dirty and threadbare. I closed my eyes tightly. I wanted to remember that moment. It was irony—beautiful and sparkling, because it was surely not the most wonderful time of the year for any of us.

The doctor I had been seeing didn't work weekends, so I was seen by two other doctors. Both of them casually opened my file on their computers in my room and let out a gasp. Both of them told me that prescribing an antidepressant to me during my first stay was a big no-no. Both of them told me it would take months for my brain chemistry to become regulated. I stayed in the unit until I was safe. It took six long days for most of the suicidal thoughts to leave me. During that time I felt heavy and drugged, but I wasn't scared of myself anymore. I'll never forget how the December air felt on my face when I stepped outside to go home. I thought that maybe I would be okay after all.

CHRISTMAS

In my unwavering hope, I latched onto the idea that if I could just make it to a beach, I would feel better, I would feel safe. Noah booked a last-minute condo in Charleston, South Carolina, and the five of us made the four hour drive the day after I got out of the psych unit. I gazed out of my window at the setting sun and took a picture of my hand reaching for it. "Hope," Noah posted on Instagram that night. We held onto it.

The condo was on the seventh floor, and I held my breath and closed my eyes as we walked by the outside railings where I could see the drop below. Snapshots of myself falling filled my mind, and I squeezed my eyes tighter. That night, we watched *Miracle on 34th Street*, then put the kids to bed. Even though I was drugged and sleepy, the balcony beckoned to me. I walked out and looked at the pool below and the patch of concrete directly underneath me. I backed away. We dragged the outdoor furniture inside and barricaded the sliding glass door. I paced and wept and shook with fear while Noah slept peacefully.

We spent the next morning on the beach. It was chilly, and I lay face down in the cold sand like a wet blanket was covering me. I was fresh out of my third hospitalization, feeling beaten. Abused. Drugged. There's a picture Noah snapped with his phone to send to a friend who asked how I was doing. It shows my two-year-old daughter leaning over me, her hand gently placed on my body, willing me, begging me to get up. Where had her mama gone? No matter how much I wanted to get up, I could not. My heart was yearning for connection, for play. I wanted my children to feel safe. I wanted their playful mama to come back. She just wasn't there. I couldn't find her anywhere.

The beach didn't heal me.

As if I were driving through a heavy fog, my short Christmas season was a blur. It was a tornado of joy and sadness. Christmas Eve, I drove to church to play violin in the service, just like I had always done. Noah and I fought before I left, and on that big stage, looking out into the dark, empty room before service began, I felt the urge to cut myself. I grabbed my keys, rushed behind the stage, and scratched my arm till I bled. During the service, I snuck into the kitchen and held a dull knife to my wrist, digging in but not cutting. That night was dark and terrifying, but I awoke to a bright, joyful Christmas morning with my children. I had found the perfect doll house for Lucy and filled it with thoughtful details: a tiny, green velvet couch just like ours; a great big dining room set; and the perfect family—two boys and a girl. Seeing her playing with it as the sun streamed through our windows felt like a miracle.

DON'T FIX ME

As a birth doula, I have supported countless mothers as they work their way through the miraculous birth process. Most of the time I can help; I can squeeze hips or apply a cold cloth to her head. But there is a point in labor when delivery is near, where all hands come off and all we can do is wait. I crouch nearby and watch as mama is deep in her own world. I can try to do small things here and there, but mostly I have to surrender the desire to control the situation. I have to wait. I have to sit on my hands and resist the urge to fix her; because through the pain comes the birth. I need only watch it unfold, whispering, "I'm here. You're not alone."

Not being able to fix things is uncomfortable. Much of the time it is excruciating. In suffering, things can't be fixed. Not truly, not wholly. Because of this, people don't know how to show up. But this I know for sure: people want to.

After my first miscarriage, I was bombarded with people who meant well, saying things that really didn't help.

"At least it was only at twelve weeks. My friend lost her baby at thirty-two weeks."

"At least you have another baby to hold."

"God has another baby for you."

"Something was probably really wrong with the baby. It would have been deformed."

"God never makes mistakes."

"This, too, shall pass."

You know what really reached my heart during that time? My friend Monique showing up at my house with a pot of spaghetti and sitting by me silently. She didn't try to fix me, she didn't even ask if we liked spaghetti (we don't), but she came and she sat with me in my sadness.

That first experience of a supportive presence gave me a freedom to love others in their pain. I don't ever worry about doing the perfect thing, because I know there is no such thing.

Sometimes I drop ice cream off on their front porch or engrave their baby's name on a bracelet to remember them. Sometimes I fold clothes or bring a meal. I never ask. I just do. I do because I know that when they are deep in pain, people can't ask for what they need because they do not know what to ask for. I certainly do not bring God and His will into the equation. I usually hug them or sit with them and say, "I'm so sorry." And oftentimes I say, with tears in my eyes, "This sucks." There are no perfect words. There don't even have to be words at all. There is nothing new to say that will miraculously heal the loss of someone's son. There is nothing to say to someone dying of cancer that will take away the ache. We can't fix pain. We can do all the small things to try to support others with food, childcare, or money, but we can't wipe it away. So show up. Don't even ask. Hurting people need to hear your whisper, "I'm here. You're not alone."

SHOWING UP

How to show up for someone who is hurting:

- Make them a music playlist.
- Send them a single song.
- Pack the kids' lunches for the week.
- Show up in your pajamas to take them for a ride in the car just as they are.
- Leave ice cream on their porch with a notification text.
- Brush their hair.
- Gently guide them into the sun or into the woods for free, outdoor therapy.
- Wave at their window.
- Send them nonperishable snacks.
- Send them tacos. Always tacos.
- Clean out their fridge and freezer since they are usually overflowing with food going bad.
- Give them a living plant.
- Present them with a soft blanket.
- Provide support and love for the caregiver.
- Give them a pretty, brightly painted rock.

- Send them a text with "Coffee at the back door!"
- Sit in the waiting room when they're at the doctor's office or hospital, even though they might not see you.
- Tell them how wonderful they are, looking deep into their eyes.
- Show up for childcare.
- Write their lost loved one's name on something. Engrave it on a necklace. Write it in the sand.
- Watch a movie with them, curled up on the couch in silence.
- Take a walk with them.
- Take their laundry home and return it, clean and folded.
- Tuck money into in an envelope and leave it for them as a surprise.
- Host them at your house (a way for them to get out while staying in).
- If you know them well, help to get them in the shower or bath.
- Buy them new underwear.
- Send them gift cards.
- Run an errand for them, picking up meds, paper towels, dry cleaning.
- Replace staple food items like milk or coffee.
- Put food in their mouth. Sit next to them and gently feed them.
- Invite them to a dinner out with friends. Something fun; normalcy!
- Choose an appropriate moment to talk about yourself to help lift the weight of their current reality and distract from the intensity of their situation.
- Give them a vase of wildflowers.

- Present them with lovely printed photographs.
- Send them a card in the mail.
- Provide them with art supplies.
- Buy them new pajamas.
- Take their kids to the park.
- Lie with them until they fall asleep.
- Take them to get their hair done.
- Send them daily texts simply saying, "I'm here. Checking in." without expecting anything in return.
- Put your hand on their back, not saying a thing.
- Cry with them, not saying a thing.
- Do something creative with them.
- Give them back rubs.
- Show up and clean their toilet—clean anything.
- Read them poetry, verses, or a favorite book.
- Speak the name of the person they are mourning.
- Set reminders to remember the anniversary of an event that's meaningful to them.
- Show up days, weeks, months, and years after everyone else stops.

MANIA

After Christmas, I sat in my psychiatrist's office and asked to be taken off the heavy antipsychotics that were suppressing the life out of me. I was afraid. Afraid of descending down into that scary place again. Afraid of losing control. Still, I asked and he agreed. A little at a time, we switched over to a new med, and my side effects were reduced. Not long afterwards, I felt the flush of life return to my cheeks, and I was hopeful. I became productive, I felt bits of joy, and I started feeling connected to my children and in my relationships for the first time in forever.

Then it began. It started with my sleep. I stayed awake later and later each night, until the evenings bled into the morning hours. I would pace the house, wringing my hands and willing the sun to come up. I busied myself with organizing and putting my house back together after I had been sick for so long. I couldn't hold a conversation for long, but I could organize every drawer and closet in the house. One day, my mother helped me clean out my van, and I squealed in excitement when I saw the laundry baskets of random things that needed to be put away. The action of putting things in their places felt like a brain massage, and I needed that badly. Soon my hands couldn't keep up with my mind. My thoughts were racing at superhuman speed, reminding me of before.

But I wasn't hallucinating, I wasn't plagued with suicidal thoughts, and I wasn't oppressed with darkness. I did puzzles, savoring the control I felt. I was completing one-thousand-piece puzzles in a single day as the mania overtook my body.

I paced around the house, feeling like my skin was being burned with acid. A heartbeat of energy pulsed through my body as if I had just hiked to the top of a mountain. One night, during the long hours I was awake as Noah was snoring, I suddenly felt the ability to open my brain in such a way that I could see my entire house in one glance: every room, the corners of my junk drawer, and everything in between. A cracked water bottle top prompted me to go online and order a replacement from Amazon. While there, I ordered a missing earring back, hangers that didn't match, and a deep fryer. Hours later, after scouring the house in my mind, I had ordered dozens of items, including two mattresses. Hitting the "Place your order" button gave me escape, and when I felt my house was complete, I was finally able to rest for a few moments.

I couldn't eat. I felt like food fueled the awful energy bubbling inside me. I remember seeing a mint on the table and covering my face with my arms as if blocking a grenade. My favorite salad could undo me. It felt like my body would split open and I could die.

One day, it was so windy the trees were bending over in submission. I watched them from behind my window, safe in my warm home. In desperation, I walked outside in my underwear, arms outstretched, head bent into the wind. The force matched the intensity inside me, and I felt temporary relief. Still, tears froze on my cheeks. The hope and goodness I had felt days earlier had vanished, and here I was again.

"Please help me," I texted Amy.

Amy arrived within the hour. I was delirious, and as she talked to me on my worn brown couch, Lucy came and sat on my lap. I immediately jumped up with a yell. It felt like she had peed all over me, but it was just her body heat that had drenched my lap like hot oil. Amy laid out a big blanket on the floor, and I crawled on top of it. She wrapped me up in it like a newborn baby, tight and safe. I thrashed a bit as fear rose in my chest, but slowly the energy diminished to the point where my body felt calm. She called my doctor for different meds while I lay there panting.

For the next few days, Noah had to leave work several times a day to swaddle me. Those were some of the most tender moments of our marriage for me. We waited for me to swing again, away from that awful manic state. Within four days the new meds started their work, and my brilliant mind burned out like a shooting star. I wouldn't wish mania on my worst enemy.

JUST COME TO ME SO
I'M NOT ALONE

Tears, come and wash me clean.
Come and shatter the dream.

Come and soothe my burning skin.
Come, make me me again.

Come, water my grave,
Come, hydrate my bones.

Just come to me so I'm not alone.

WINTER SEA

When the new year came, it was like we were all leaving a nightmare behind. There were brief moments where I felt nearly normal. "Normal" was like a tightrope that I balanced on for a brief moment each time I swung to the left or right. But in between normal, I faked it. I committed to taking every step forward to heal, but I couldn't heal unless I pretended.

It was decided by the people surrounding me, after the feelings of crisis had faded a bit, that a week at the beach would be good for me. A chance to get away. A cleansing. A year before I had photographed a wedding, and my payment was a week at a beach house right on the ocean. Noah couldn't be there the first part of the week, and I certainly could not be alone yet, so my sister Julianna, with her thirty-eight-week ripe belly and all the aches that come with that, would come with her one-year-old daughter, and I would bring Lucy. I should have been caring for her, but instead she was caring for me.

The night before we left, I found myself hunched over my sink, staring deep into my eyes in the mirror. I saw something frightening in them, something new. In a panic, I reached for some scissors and slashed off my long braid. Before it hit the floor I regretted it. I was flooded with the realization that I could do other things that scared me. *I could kill myself.*

The next day, all of my sisters came to my home. There were whispers as I sat there in shame with my mutilated hair. A mama close to her due date, a woman on the brink of another breakdown, and two babies were not ideal travel companions. I promised I would be good— as if any of it was in my control. I needed to escape my home with all its haunting memories. I needed to be far away from the knives and from the staircase that sent shudders down my spine every time I glanced at it. I spent weeks walking by the stairs with my back pressed against the wall, holding my breath until I had passed the place I had seen myself drop and die, where I had seen a pile of my children.

In the end, it was decided that we would risk it. We piled in the van with my sister's giant belly smashed up against the wheel. We laughed, and the closer we got to the coast, the louder our laughter got. It felt like coming out of a black cave into the warm light. It was the safest I had felt for almost a year.

The cozy cottage where we stayed at was old but clean. There wasn't much light inside except for what came through the large window that faced the sea—light that bathed us in the softest glow. I spent the days walking on the beach, reading, sleeping, painting, writing, doing puzzles, and typing on my typewriter. My obsessions had turned from death to poetry. I spent hours researching writers and reading their work. I typed moving quotes onto bits of torn paper. I read a lot of Sylvia Plath poems and ended up ordering forty different books by and about her on eBay. Most assuredly, she was not the best author for me to binge on at that time. Plath wrote her poems and her quintessential book, *The*

Bell Jar, as a depressed woman and committed suicide in 1963. But my curiosity about her work and life felt like movement forward.

My sister took care of the girls in spurts so I could write. In the evenings, after the girls had gone to bed, she would read *Anne of Green Gables* aloud to me as I did puzzles, and when we were in bed she sang to me softly until I fell asleep.

I love a winter beach. I love how clean it is, stripped of bodies and colored towels. I love how the wind echoes the waves and how I feel sandwiched between them. When I wasn't writing, we would bundle up to go play in the sand. We laughed as the girls toddled around in their bulky coats and fed the birds. I lay with my face in the sand, resting. It felt like a womb. I couldn't remember anything so lovely.

Noah came the second half of the week and brought our two energetic boys. My sister left and went on to deliver her baby girl less than two weeks later.

Being with my family wasn't quite as gentle as being with my sister, but it was still absolutely wonderful. I watched the children climb the dunes and play in the tide pools. I lay in the sand, face to the sea, and welcomed kisses and hugs every time the kids brought them. We didn't say very much, and in the stillness, waves of grief for what our family had lost came over me. I didn't know how things would ever be the same, and I mourned the loss of my joy. It felt stolen. But for that week, I just closed my eyes and let the sea soothe it all.

STRINGS

I returned home from the beach with a longing for normalcy, and it seemed like things were getting there. I was alone with the kids for the first time in months. I packed their lunches. I went to therapy. But I did it all with my mask back on. I hid the disgusting thoughts that were creeping back in, but I couldn't do it for long. Days crawled by, and I started losing my grip again. My obsession with death started pulsing through my body, gaining strength daily. The nights were once more long and lonely. Knives and meds were hidden. I couldn't be with the children alone. I remember lying on the couch watching the babysitter interact with them, and it felt foreign to me.

The visions of the past few months were branded into me—every detail vibrant and live. I scrawled in my journal:

I am terrified of homeless men. Every corner I turn I'm expecting to see their haggard bodies leaning against the wall.

Will they find me? Will they hunt me down?

Will they lean down over my children and breathe in their sleeping faces?

Will they choke me in my sleep?

Will they wake me from my imagination with a plea for food or drugs?

I can smell them.

I can see them.

I can hear their mumbling sexual fantasies.

They will find me.

They will take me back.

They will rape me.

They will make me drink their spit.

I don't think that I will ever not be terrified.

I started having an obsession about my middle child, Sullivan. Sullivan was my snuggler. We had a special bond, different from the other two. Instead of snuggling with me, he started transforming day by day in front of my eyes, losing his softness and warmth. He was gaining weight, his pants could not button, and he would cry for hours at night because he wanted us lying right next to him. One day at lunch he looked at me coldly and said, "Why don't you kill yourself?" Soon after, I saw a flash in my mind of Sullivan tied up in a wet basement somewhere, struggling to get free of the rope tying him down. I looked at the boy in front of me and was certain he was not my son. Maybe he was a demon in disguise. I kept this thought to myself for days while observing him. I saw more flashes of Sullivan tied up in that basement, screaming for me. I had to stab the demon to set my son free. I told Noah this, and they took the kids away to my mama's house. I was relieved.

One desperate afternoon I asked my pastor to meet with me. We sat outside a coffee shop, all bundled up, watching the town stroll by. I told him about Sullivan. "I need to get the real Sullivan back," I said.

"There is no demon, Helen Joy," he said, gently but firmly.

I asked him questions about the universe and about where God was—because it didn't feel like He was with me. He said things I don't recall, but I do remember him saying that God holds the strings of the universe. The earth is the perfect distance from the sun to keep us warm and grow food. Any closer, we would burn; any farther, we would freeze.

Two nights later, in the wee morning hours, I ran outside in the snow wearing only my nightgown and slippers and walked for miles in the bad parts of town, mentally willing someone to shoot me. As I stared at the moon, I saw it melt before my eyes just like the wax of a candle. Immediately, I texted my pastor, "The moon is melting. God let go of the strings."

The strings of the world had been released, and the earth was bouncing through the cosmos like a giant ball. I couldn't get a grip no matter how hard I tried, no matter what medicines they tried. Whispers of me going somewhere for long-term care started growing into a frightening shout in my mind. I waved my white flag. I would go.

GIVING UP

In all the months of darkness, I imagined there had to be a real place for healing somewhere in this country. I believed it was real but thought it was just too much money or would require too much time away from my family. By the time I agreed to treatment, I was ravenous for it. The only thing holding me back was that I would miss Sullivan's birthday. The thought of abandoning him destroyed me, but I finally made the decision to go.

My mama held my hand and pleaded for me to not leave my children. "They need you," she said. She promised to help more and nurse me back to health. But I said no. I just couldn't do it anymore. She got angry. My therapist met with her and explained that I was very sick, just like if I had diabetes or cancer. I know she didn't understand, but she eventually got behind me.

As friends and family members started calling facilities to try to find a place for me, I had two conditions. First, I wanted the ability to be outside. The thought of being locked up again made me feel sick. Second, I didn't want to be anywhere near a man. Even without those conditions, it was hard to find a place. Since I didn't struggle with addiction, there just weren't that many treatment centers that would take me. I didn't have an eating disorder, I wasn't a sex addict, I didn't do drugs, I wasn't an alcoholic. I felt like an island.

One place was perfect, except they allowed only one hour of outside time in a courtyard per day. Other places were booked for several weeks out, required three months of commitment, cost a hundred thousand dollars, or were addiction-based. Each minute that passed reminded us all that I needed immediate care. It was maddening. Once again, I started getting that panicked feeling that no one was going to take care of me.

After a day of research, we finally found a women-only facility in Florida that dealt with mental health in addition to addiction. On their website I saw that patients could walk to the river and watch the sunset every night after dinner. It sounded too good to be true. We started the registration process and began making plans and getting ready to pack. I was questioned for an hour by a team, from the facility, who asked every intimate question there was. My home was swarming with people checking in on me and helping me. Minutes before confirming my flight to Florida, we received a phone call.

"We are so sorry, but after our specialist reviewed your chart he has decided that you are too critical for us. We cannot care for you."

The bottom dropped out. I couldn't stop crying. Here I was again.

Not long after that, they called back and told us about their sister facility in the mountains of Tennessee. The man we talked to there had a voice so smooth it was like silk. He oozed compassion and once in a while seemed choked up with emotion as I told my story. He said they had a bed available for me that week in a home for women like me who weren't addicts. This place boasted of outdoor and equine therapy, and the online schedule included mindful eating and yoga. He promised, several times, that the men on campus would not be near me. He painted a picture of sisters cooking a healthy dinner together in the kitchen. And best of all, families could visit! These phrases dripped out of his lips like honey, and I lapped them right up.

We bartered with him to try and get the price down as low as we could. I calculated the cost of staying in the nicest hotel in our city instead, with the necessary amenities, and having my friends take shifts to keep me alive. Although that would have been much cheaper than the facility, it wasn't safer, and deep down we all knew that.

Once the plans were in place and my airline ticket had been purchased, I had only two days. There was much to prepare, but I was still being constantly bombarded with hallucinations and suicidal ideations, so those two days suspended me in a sort of purgatory. I didn't want to go, and I couldn't wait to. That evening I was at our local Fresh Market, looking for something to eat for dinner, when I was struck by a bunch of yellow tulips sitting in a bin. Sunshine. Hope. I was disarmed by their beauty, and my heart was pricked by memories of a woman I barely remembered—that beautiful new bride I once was who had clutched yellow tulips to her breast. I placed the flowers in my basket, aching for the hope they represented. At the end of my shopping trip, I sorrowfully returned them to their bucket of water. Although I longed to take them home with me and let their sunshine fill my home, I was leaving the next day and knew their beauty would be long gone before I returned.

For brief moments, my obsessions moved from death to silly details I felt needed to be settled before I left. Who would make Sullivan's birthday cupcakes for his class? Who would help the kids address their valentines? What if my family ran out of toilet paper or cereal? What if my sick grandmother died while I was gone and I never got the four-generation photograph I had been putting off for a year?

Friends and family rallied around me, each taking a bit of the burden. A friend promised to make and deliver the birthday cupcakes. My sister-in-law promised to fill out valentines with the kids. A meal train was set up for my family. I took pictures with my grandmother. A lump grew in my throat as I hugged her goodbye. She was quite sick, but so was I.

Mama took me to Target the day before I left. I couldn't even drive, I was so sick. Since most of my wardrobe was skirts, I had to buy pants for the horseback riding and rock climbing I was expecting to do there. I also wanted to purchase household staples to make life easier for Noah. I felt emaciated as I leaned over the cart and trudged down the aisles. I shuffled along in my slippers and filled two carts with Chex cereal, toilet paper, and lots of stationery to write home with. Mama bought me a beautiful floral set of PJs just like she had before each of my births. I picked out pants so wide and so ugly it felt like I was going away to camp. Later that evening, I stopped to grab something at the grocery store and saw a six-foot-tall Star Wars stormtrooper balloon. As I stood there looking up at it, tears flooded me. I wanted my boy to have that for his birthday, and I couldn't be there to give it to him. I texted my mom a picture, and I knew she would make it happen.

When the children had been put to bed and I kissed them for the last time, I made videos for each of them, singing them lullabies with my voice cracking and my face contorted to try to keep from crying. I hoped that if they were sad or scared Noah could play them for them. I sang happy birthday to Sullivan and told him his birth story. It took ten takes to get one that sounded happy. I wanted him to be happy, not sad. Numbness replaced the faucet of feelings I usually had as I wrote his sixth-birthday letter. I wrapped presents and valentines. I lined up the cereal and toilet paper on a table in my hall like little lines of army men ready for battle.

As I was packing the last of my things into my suitcase, I collapsed onto the bathroom floor, shaking with fear and emotion. The ache was growing in the pit of my stomach. I was despondent that I had to leave my children—again. I was afraid of being alone. Noah couldn't handle my emotions. I yelled and screamed at him, begging for connection, but I pushed him away and he left me crying on the floor. The familiar chill that I first felt when he turned his back on me when I was cheering back in high school overtook me again. He went to bed early, and I was left to try to stay alive just one more night. I walked the rooms of my house, searching for my hidden meds, wanting to hold them in my hands and tempt fate. When the sun finally rose, a bit of hope rose in me as well. Maybe my salvation was waiting for me in Tennessee.

THEY FORGOT ME

Summer took me to the airport early that morning. Before I left, Noah handed me the meds that he had been hiding in a brown paper bag and gave me a side hug. I hung my head in shame as I climbed into the car, and we drove away. The ride was eerily quiet. As I boarded the plane, I could feel everyone in our small town exhaling in relief that they didn't have to deal with me for a while.

As the plane took off, my brain started coming apart. There were so many new ways to die, I thought I might vomit. I closed my eyes so tight that all I could see was that bunch of yellow tulips from the grocery store.

The plan was for me to land and head straight for baggage claim, where I would be picked up by a staff member. Noah had checked with them three times to make sure they would be there so I wouldn't have to wait. I just had to make it there, and I would be safe.

As I walked to the exit, my full bottle of lithium burned a hole in the backpack. I wanted to take all of them right there in the airport bathroom and save everyone the trouble of trying to put me back together. Like a toddler, I took one small step in front of the other until I made it to the escalator. I scanned the faces below, looking for a kind-eyed woman. I didn't see her. I searched for anyone looking for me or holding a sign with my name. There was no one. No one was there for me. Panicking,

I called Noah, who was told that they had forgotten me and would send someone from the facility—which was more than an hour away. It was a cruel welcome.

The hour I had to wait seemed like days. I didn't feel safe and wrote in my journal to occupy my mind. I made lists. I wrote about the yellow tulips. I didn't dare glance toward the bathroom, where I could see my dead body slumped over the toilet. He finally came. *He.* The man was short and gruff, triggering all my traumas from the men in the first hospital. His presence betrayed the promise I had been given that I wouldn't have to be around men. I shook in my seat the entire drive, which took two hours instead of one because a semitruck wreck blocked most of the highway. I kept closing my eyes and seeing the beautiful green fields from the brochures, telling myself that when I got there I would be able to breathe.

Fortunately, the driver turned out to be nice. He worked with the men in the sex addiction home, and I could tell he wasn't used to talking to women like me. Near the end of our ride, he mentioned a place called Piney—a locked-down hospital of sorts where you have to be observed for several days before they let you go into the homes. This was where drug and alcohol detoxes took place for both men and women. I begged him not to take me there. My trauma was repeating, like I was stuck in a loop of horrors.

We pulled up to a beautiful log building. Behind it lay a vast landscape of green with bones of a teepee on it. The picture of healing. The vision of the Native American woman that had saved me in the hospital flooded me. The check-in process was gentle, and I was soothed by the deep southern accents of the attendants. The admissions building was clean and modern, and I could see why the cost to go there was so hefty. I sat there while they rummaged through my things, removing items that weren't allowed. I was told that they'd bring my things to my room, and I was escorted to Piney for my observation.

Just the short walk across the lawn brought me from luxury to what felt like a clinic from the 1970s. Worn linoleum and wood veneer made everything look dirty and dull. As they locked the door behind me, I looked over my shoulder at the fields outside and sighed.

After I was questioned, poked, and prodded, I was shown to my room, which basically consisted of two beds and a small dresser. A shared bathroom connected the room to another room. It was dark. All of the furniture was dark brown and very little light came through the small windows. I sat on the bed, unsure of what to do. Finally someone told me to come eat a lunch that they had warmed up for me. A country woman missing most of her teeth happily handed it to me. Next, I was told to go to group therapy down the hall. As I peered in, I saw five men sitting there. I wanted to run and hide, but I knew there was nowhere to go. I crossed my arms over my breasts and sat in a corner. We went around the circle, introducing ourselves. Every one of the men was there for sex addiction. I couldn't find the words to even describe why I was there and ended up in a mess of tears. When I got back to my room, someone had brought my things to me, but they were strewn about the closet like it had been ransacked. I rummaged through and noticed that many items were missing.

"They took my dress," I wrote in my journal.

They took my dress. The one that I had clung to during every hospital stay ever since I was forced to wear paper scrubs eight inches too long. It was soft and feminine with wildflowers printed on it. The dress represented my humanity. It was a reminder that I was Helen Joy. They took every dress that made me *me,* and I was left with a pile of ugly, black jersey, plus-sized pants. I found out a month later it was because they didn't have sleeves.

I got to go outside when the smokers smoked. Sitting on a picnic table nearby, I enjoyed the feeling of air on my face but felt like a prisoner being let out into the yard. I was not allowed to use the phone, so I wrote two desperate letters to Noah. I ached with loneliness and fell asleep that night with my arms wrapped around myself.

The second day, I was awakened early by a man sticking his head through my door—a blatant disregard of my privacy and feelings of safety—telling me to come for breakfast. I jumped out of bed and headed in my PJs to the kitchen, where I sat at a table by myself since I was the only woman. The table of men were joking and laughing and enjoying their meal. I kept my eyes down.

The day had me ricocheting between feelings of relief and despair. I attended two group sessions and I started to warm up to the men, realizing that they weren't out to get me, they were longing for wholeness, just like me. Halfway through the day, a girl detoxing from drugs joined us. She was mean and curled up on the couch with her head down. She was put in the room attached to the other side of the bathroom, and I heard her throwing up several times.

I paced the halls, studying the childlike posters that had grown crusty with time. They were hand-drawn in crayon and were about eating disorders. As I dragged my fingers over the beige-painted bricks, anger started to rise in me. I was being robbed. My time and money were being stolen as I stayed locked up here where I wasn't getting treatment. I didn't know why I had to stay. I wasn't being weighed for an eating disorder or monitored for a drug detox. I was just alone again; the girl without visible symptoms. I didn't want to start a puzzle because that felt like surrender, so instead I filled my journal with angry words.

Finally, in the late afternoon I was seen by an older man, a doctor. We spent two hours in his office as he completed my intake exam. A student who was shadowing him sat in the corner, bright-faced and curious. As I rattled off my story the doctor became fascinated by me. Excited even. He said he wanted to help me, and hope began to rise from the dark place where I had pushed it down. This man was smart, and I felt like if I were under his care, all this waiting would be worth it. I never saw him again.

Right before dinner, a woman told me to get my things ready immediately because I was being placed in a house. She gave me a pink lanyard with a blurry picture of myself on it and said, "You're in the trauma house."

They loaded me into a big white van, and I was off. We drove ten minutes through winding country roads. Trauma house. It kind of blindsided me. It was the first time I had felt someone had named my stuff as it should have been named. I scratched at my arms as we pulled up to a big, beautiful home with a circular driveway out front. It was red brick with white columns, and as we climbed the stairs I noticed a pile of mismatched shoes to the left.

We walked into the small, dark living room, and the first thing I saw was a girl with a radiant and pleasant face doing a puzzle. I exhaled. It was such a familiar sight to me. Women were napping on the couch, piled high with blankets. I was left standing there while they gave my suitcase to the RA to go through it again. I heard commotion from the kitchen where a woman was having a fit about some Oreo balls they were making. It was the weekly dessert night, the only night we were allowed sugar, and it made all the girls a little feral. I sat in a chair and took it all in. The place seemed dirty. It was cluttered, with shelves stuffed with random things, pictures that were framed crooked, an ironic "Live. Laugh. Love." sign, and a broken oven. A young girl with a cascade of brown curls and bright eyes sat with me and explained the detailed rules of the house—and there were a lot of them.

I sat at the long table for dinner and took in the faces of the women around it. Normal, beautiful faces. The women took turns introducing themselves and told me why they were there. When it ended with me, I quietly said, "I'm Helen Joy, and I'm here for bipolar disorder, suicidal ideations, and self harm." And just like that, I was welcomed into the sisterhood.

They had seated me next to a woman with dissociative identity disorder. Next to her legs lay a tiny therapy dog. She spent dinner talking like a little girl and saying the sweetest, most hilarious things. With no warning, she bolted out of the house and tried to run into the woods. It was chaos. They finally caught her and tried to take her back to Piney. The other girls rebelled and screamed at the RA and the nurse to let her stay. One of them threatened to attempt suicide so she could go with her. I kept my head down and willed myself to disappear. I did not like it there after all.

TREATMENT

My stay at treatment can be summed up in two words: anger rising. The whole time I was there felt like I was perpetually living in my childlike self. The little girl under the bed who no one came for; the teenager with a doll. A familiar feeling came creeping in, one of deep loneliness and pain.

It became clear within the first few days that the empathetic man on the phone with the voice like velvet had never been to this place. Mindful breakfast every day consisted of rushing to the table with a bowl of sugary cereal and slumping over in your chair while not talking for fifteen minutes. We cooked together, but because our day was so packed with groups, we usually had one hour to cook for fifteen or more people. The oven did not work properly the whole time I was there, making cooking complicated and laborious. It was temperamental, and the temperature fluctuated. Sometimes we ate undercooked pasta and other times burned pizza. Once a week, we sat around and ordered groceries auction-style, holding up three fingers if we wanted three apples, raising our hand to express the percentage of fat we liked in our milk. While there were veggies and fruits available, many of the women ate frozen, premade meals. At lunchtime lines would form as everyone watched the glowing microwave in a trance. I thought to myself, *This wasn't on the website.*

The first Sunday I was there, we loaded up in white vans to go to church. A group of girls went to a group called Spirituality, where they watched a movie while sprawled out on the floor in a small, dark room. I followed another group as they filed into a different building for church. I saw men—men that I was promised I wouldn't see. They sat on the left of the room, and the women sat across on the right. It looked like an old-fashioned Quaker meeting. We weren't to even lock eyes with them, so I hung my head down as I sat in my seat. Church started with an old timey song, "I'll Fly Away."

Some bright morning when this life is over
I'll fly away
To that home on God's celestial shore
I'll fly away

I'll fly away, oh glory
I'll fly away in the morning
When I die, hallelujah by and by
I'll fly away

My body grew hot, my face flushed. I looked around in shock. This was a suicide song. It celebrated dying; it shined it up like an antique car. I refused to say the words. Instead, I sat down on my chair and reached under it, searching for metal. I found a rough piece and rubbed it on my wrists, rocking back and forth to the beat. I didn't press hard enough to draw blood.

On the van ride home I watched a seat belt next to the door swinging and clanking as we curved around the turns. It taunted me. I felt like I could wrap it around my neck and open the sliding door. Then it would be over.

I had been told to tell the RA any time I had bad thoughts. So as soon as we got back from church I went to the RA on call and told her some of my thoughts. She took me to the freezer and took out a frozen orange and handed it to me to hold. The cold didn't wake me from the visions. We went for a walk. When we returned, there was a woman waiting for me. She had been assigned to me for twenty-four hours and had to be by my side the entire time. She stood outside my door when I peed and showered, and I wasn't allowed to sleep in my bed. Instead, I was given a couch made up as a bed where she watched me sleep. I fell asleep with that old country song filling my head. *I'll fly away.* I wanted to fly away, but I was determined to work on staying.

I couldn't call my family. There was a strict phone policy that included levels you had to reach in order to use it. Level ones couldn't use the phone at all; level twos could use it for twenty minutes, three times a week; and level threes could use it every day. Even in a hospital, I had free use of the phone and constant connection to my family, but here I was cut off. I begged everyone to let me call my son on his birthday. On Valentine's Day evening, right around the time I had given birth to him, an RA took me outside and let me call Sullivan. I didn't want to say "happy birthday" but instead wanted to scream, "Save me!" into the receiver. I quieted the voices in my head and listened to Sullivan ramble about the birthday party I was missing.

A day or two later, I was allowed to call Noah from my therapist's office. She was working on the computer while I talked, and I could only see the back of her head, but I knew she was listening. I gave short yes and no answers to his questions, afraid that the truth would burst from me. When she left the room for a few brief moment, I whispered madly, "It's not like they said here! Don't pay the second half of the deposit. Oh, God, please get me out!"

I spoke on the phone a grand total of one hundred eighty minutes that month. Each call was spent in the presence of an RA and countless other women from the house. I could never say what I wanted to, and my clues and codes were never picked up by the person on the other end. Instead, I wrote the truths and the lies in letters and mailed them. Somehow, the mail was so slow that for weeks after I returned home I received letters from myself.

The women in the house were intense and woven with deep trauma. Some of them had a layer of addiction covering it. There were entitled college students with mounds of crocheting draped over their laps. I giggled as I watched them, unable to picture them at a college party on the outside. There were two mothers other than myself, and there were women who had to care for themselves instead of having children. My best friend in the house was a bright, smart woman who made me laugh. She was a recovering crack addict with major depressive disorder who had lost custody of her children and was riddled with childhood trauma. We did laps around the driveway every day, and my love for her felt decades old. The collective sexual trauma in the house was like a tidal

YELLOW TULIPS · 237

wave. I felt repeatedly battered by the horrific details, and I felt, once again, alone. My stories of hospitals and psychosis felt silly compared with the suffering these women had been through. Every hour of every day, I struggled to minimize my pain. It was as if I was embarrassed to take up space.

My whole life, I have been painfully empathetic. I constantly poured myself out for others and willingly filled myself up with their hurt. I was not able to function like that in the house. The sheer emotional needs would have drowned me in a minute. Nearly every second of the day a woman was having a panic attack or sobbing in someone's arms. There was never a break. One night before dinner four women were crying at the same time. I stood there watching them all, and I didn't go to them. I snuck outside in the cold and lay on the pavement, staring at the stars. I realized I could not hold the pain for them, and I finally let go. This was a gift, the ability to separate myself from pain and suffering. It's a gift I took home with me.

On many evenings and on Sundays we were carted around to local Alcoholics and Narcotics Anonymous meetings. One Sunday everyone, addicts and nonaddicts alike, took an hour-long bus ride to a small Baptist church in a town that was so small I didn't see the name. I found myself at a Narcotics Anonymous meeting, sitting on the dirty floor of the fellowship hall. We were packed in, two layers deep, a mixture of men and women. My heart was pounding as everyone went around the room, saying their name and why they were there.

"Hi, I'm Jim and I'm a coke addict. I was sober for three months but now I'm back."

"Hi, I'm Kit and this is my first meeting. I'm a crack addict."

When it got to me, I didn't stop crocheting and simply said "Hi, I'm Helen Joy."

What the hell was I doing there? I had never even experimented with drugs, and now I was forced to sit in a room filling my mind with stories of relapse? I identified closely with the despair and the loneliness, but the fact that I paid well over a thousand dollars to be treated for just that one day weighed heavily on me. Some girls who didn't necessarily need the meetings were satisfied with the box of donuts that was passed around. I went to a lot of meetings, filled out a lot of twelve-step sheets, learned the lingo. Despite my resistance, I still learned. I still grew. I found the despair and loneliness in my own heart mirrored back to me from them. In the end, I stopped separating myself from them.

Every day I awaited the mail like a starving person. The RA would come into the house office with her arms piled high with packages and letters, and we would all line up, trying to be patient. Each letter and package had to be opened and checked for contraband. Books had to be approved, toiletries had to be inspected for alcohol content. One day a package from my mom arrived, and inside of it was a bottle of beer conditioner—hair conditioner that was made with a high concentration of . . . beer. I laughed until I cried. My mother had sent alcohol to rehab, and I loved her for it. Of course they took it away and my hair continued to tangle, but my heart was so glad for that moment of hilarity. Some days I wouldn't get any mail, and other days I would receive ten letters at a time from friends and family, many of whom I didn't even realize knew I was there. I treasured them. I read and reread every detail and clutched them to my chest. My mom was the best. She just told me normal, everyday things and sent pictures. She once described in detail how she went to get the giant stormtrooper balloon the night before Sullivan's birthday. The store was filled with bleary-eyed men looking for a last-minute Valentines' Day gift for their wives or girlfriends. While she was standing in line to check out, a man with a thick country accent asked her about her valentine. She replied, with her arm around the balloon, "He doesn't talk much." I burst into laughter and shared the story with the other girls. I still have a box of those letters from that month stashed in my closet. Oxygen in a box.

Despite what the admissions office would have you believe, the campus and housing were spread over many miles. Some days we would spend hours in the vans, going to and from appointments and events. Every time we loaded into the vans, the chatter stopped and we all listened to the radio, rocked into a trance by the music we couldn't listen to anywhere else and the curve of the Tennessee mountain roads. Once in a while, a song would come on that we couldn't help but dance to. The whole van would erupt with all the words, and joy was in the palm of my hand. During the mundane, gray days, the van rides were a bright spot. We couldn't wait to leave our expensive group therapies so we could hear Ed Sheeran on the radio.

We called it Sunnelly, the place we had ninety percent of our group therapies. It had a double-wide feel, beige inside and out, and dirty. Harsh, yellow lights buzzed overhead. There was a pile of pillows against the wall that we sat on sometimes. Some days we found roaches in the creases. Covering the walls were posters with rules and cheesy mantras, which mocked me as I sat on the stiff chair through hours and hours of groups. Women were always draped all over the floor, snoring, tangled up in their crochet projects. I couldn't even think of sleeping over the energy and anger I possessed by just being there.

Sometimes we had our small group upstairs, when just six of us came together. We sat huddled together, surrounded by pots and pans and random items like a large lion statue; they seemed as though they belonged at a yard sale. Like the home we were staying in, Sunnelly was dirty and cluttered, as if it were an afterthought to bringing in dozens of broken women.

Some days we were in Sunnelly for eight hours straight and had to pack lunches from home. Most girls threw in a tray of frozen food since it was easy. At lunch break, women lined up like it was middle school to microwave their food in a dirty microwave that I don't think ever got cleaned the whole time I was there.

The air in that place was thick and suffocating. I watched the clock until the next break, when I would escape outside to do laps around the big tree where the smokers gathered. Afterwards, I would collapse on my back in the grass like a starfish and breath in the sweet air until I had to go back inside.

I memorized every turn to get there, and I whispered the directions to Noah during my precious twenty minutes of phone time. I begged him to write it down. I ached for him to see it when he came to get me; otherwise, he would see the grand admissions building with the beautiful wood and think that was it. I needed him to know I wasn't lying. He never ended up driving by. Some days I want to drive to Tennessee just to take him to it; then maybe he would understand.

Sometimes I fantasize about going back there. I want to break in and whitewash the whole place, stripping the old, yellowing, kindergarten-

YELLOW TULIPS • 241

like posters off of the walls. I would replace them with giant posters of mountains and rivers. I would paint weighty words about suffering and overcoming on them. I would bring in fresh flowers, two bouquets a week.

On Tuesdays we were to take off our sheets and place them in the pillowcase on the bed; in the afternoon, new ones would be waiting for us to put on. The sheets were old, and the elastic was stretched. Many times my sheets were mismatched—florals and stripes, the way I would expect at a grandmother's house. Our house was cluttered with things left behind by other girls, layered over the years. It didn't seem to be anyone's job to clear it out. Little by little during my free time, I emptied closets, threw away trauma charts, and filled bags with crusty shoes to donate to a local church. I think I was trying to make room for myself.

It was a rule that we could not be in our rooms during the day. If you wanted to nap, it had to be in the shared living room. Every day, sometimes multiple times a day, I would retreat to the shower—the only place I could be alone. I would lie on the shower floor and let the water pound out my thoughts. Sometimes I cried, but mostly I felt empty and no tears came. At night I went to bed the second I got my night meds and would fake sleep just so I could think. There were so many evenings I would lie in bed and ponder how I could go on another day. I didn't even believe that I would be better in a week. I was sure I wouldn't be better in a month. *Christmas,* I thought. *I will be better by Christmas.* I thought of Christmas, ten whole months away. I pictured myself by the tree with my children. I wanted to lie under the lights with them and sing and laugh. Yes. When things felt hopeless I would squeeze my eyes shut and think of Christmas.

After my intense feelings of self-harm were made known to the staff in those first few days of treatment, I got fast-tracked to a wonderful PA who was aggressive with my meds. She listened to me intently, often delaying her following appointment just to keep listening. She would bounce ideas off of me, and it felt like a team effort. Day by day, I regained more and more control. One day I thought there was a crow in my room, and the next I saw a white tiger standing by the road. Back I went, and the PA adjusted my meds. Then one day during a van ride, it was like someone dinged a crystal glass and a curtain fell. Everything was green. Spring was coming, and the sight of a new leaf bursting off a branch filled my body with vibrations. I thought this was good. My dark thoughts were gone and I was restored to joy. During Alcoholic Anonymous meetings I would stare at the men around me. I would watch their hands and be bombarded with images of them intertwined with their lovers. My body filled with embarrassment and delight; my cheeks flushed. One night I had the most vivid dream that I was doing laps in a pool and came to the end and saw Lucy floating lifeless, drowned. It felt more real than real life. It imprinted on my brain as if it were a true memory. I was desperate to call and make sure she was okay, but no one would let me. I cried thinking about the cherry trees blooming on my street and the finite nature of life. The absence of suicidal thoughts was glorious, but I still didn't feel like my thoughts were normal. My last meeting with the PA was a celebration, and I felt that even though I was returning home filled with more trauma from this place, at least I wanted to live.

Before entering treatment I was going to individual therapy two to three times a week at home. I was shocked to find out once I got to treatment here that I would receive exactly one fifty-minute session of individual therapy per week. A total of four sessions for my stay. My therapist was young and pretty, and she carried designer purses. I did not for one minute think she cared about me. She made me feel whiny, and she spent ninety percent of our time trying to get me to sign up for a second month of treatment. She also led our small group of five or six women in group therapy. She was all about psychodramas, which I had never had heard of before. During a psychodrama, one might address a pillow as if it were your mother who beat you, or you might act out a situation in your childhood as your adult self. I despised psychodramas. Watching a dear friend struggling to confront a scarf as if it were her rapist felt voyeuristic and inappropriate. I watched women act out all kinds of traumas. I would have tears on my cheeks, despite not wanting them there. Wet anger. It felt silly. It was a game I didn't want to play.

Halfway through my stay it was determined that I was too high risk to do any of the trauma counseling they provided. Instead, they gave me two sessions with the dialectical behavior therapist who led daily groups about coping skills. She was a bubbly woman with a kind heart. I really liked her, even though DBT skills seemed silly to me most of the time. She listened to me. She dove deep when my personal therapist didn't even scratch the surface. For our two short sessions, we focused on self-harm—what the root of it could be and how to help prevent it. *Not being seen or heard,* I wrote down.

I made a new list in my notebook:

- Draw cut marks with a red marker instead of cutting
- Stick my head in a bowl of ice water to shock me out of my panic
- Work crossword puzzles
- Knead Play-Doh
- Rub lotion on my skin to be kind to myself
- Hold a frozen orange

I felt armed for war, but she didn't think I was ready for battle.

One Tuesday, our one day to participate in outdoor therapy, I discovered that instead of being outside we were going to do an all-day psychodrama. I had been looking forward to those hours in the sun for so long, and I felt robbed. My heart ached. I spent all day hearing stories of trauma and watching them acted out. There were addiction stories, stories of neglectful parents, and a whole lot of rape stories—parents selling their children into sex slavery, incest, violent attacks. I was stuck watching it all, and I was not permitted to leave. We were given drums and shakers, misappropriating Native American storytelling traditions. It was forced and repulsive. The room was divided by black tarp that hung from the ceiling, making everything dark. Each woman acted out her story, always coming to a point of hitting, throwing, kicking, punching, cussing, screaming, or pushing, no matter how long it took. That was the goal.

I went near the beginning because I wanted it over and done with. My therapist manipulated me like a marionette, twisting and gutting me emotionally as everyone watched me and banged on the drums. She made me act out being locked up in the hospital. I didn't trust her. At one point she covered my body with a blanket and lay on top of me, goading me to get up. She wanted me to stand up for myself, to take control, but I just lay there. I didn't want to play her game. I was not having a breakthrough, and I didn't want to act like it. But I finally got up and did what she wanted so I could go back to my seat. My face was emotionless, though tears wet my cheeks, and my efforts to push her off me were weak. It was an inauthentic performance on my part.

My friend, Taylor, had her turn after me. I had felt a motherly protection over her since the moment we met, and as she went through her psychodrama she kicked and thrashed at her abuser and fell on the ground. Her pain was too much for me to bear. I banged the drum and let out an inhuman wail and started clawing at my arms in absolute panic. The red blood dripped down my arms. When I told the RA, instead of being allowed out of the room, I was given some Play-Doh to hold.

That afternoon I was made to watch as woman after woman performed. Maybe it cleansed them. It did not cleanse me.

One of the reasons I had chosen this treatment center was because it boasted a lot of outdoor time—horseback riding, rock climbing, ropes courses, and even a sweat lodge. In the month I was at treatment, I did exactly one outdoor activity: a low ropes course event; a trust exercise on a steel cable. It was the best kind of medicine to be outside doing something physical, but that was the only day for me. While many women rode horses two times a week, I hadn't saddled up by my last day there. They told me it was because I was suicidal on that first day and things got delayed, a domino effect that affected my whole stay. One afternoon before dinner, a friend snuck in a shiny new marketing brochure she had found that touted the benefits of the treatment center to possible clients. All of us pored over it, laughing at how ridiculous it was. The front showed a woman riding a horse through a river with a giant smile on her face. No helmet. The brochure made it seem like riding horses was the majority of our therapy there. My anger was rising, and an RA overheard me discussing how I was going to expose them when I got out with a scathing review about how I had not ridden a horse the whole time I was there. Before I knew it, they had arranged for someone to lead me on a horse around a small corral on my very last day.

It wasn't all bad, though. Just as tossing a ball in the halls of the psych unit months before had brought pure and bright laughter to me, there were many moments like that at treatment—pearls of goodness. On the first Saturday I was there, the new arrivals that week were taken to a room off the barn where an apple-cheeked RA gave us scraps of leather and metal stamps to make key chains and bracelets. We all hunched over on the floor: girls who were just out of jail, cowering assault survivors, rail-thin women from the eating-disorder house, women who were at the end of their rope, all hunched over, creating. The joy was breathless and unbridled. Being there with them felt like a secret. I sat back and watched them. The squeals and pride that came from even the toughest of women softened my hardening heart.

One Tuesday evening, the RAs told us we were going to have a special movie night and watch *Tangled,* the cartoon movie of Rapunzel's story. We were not allowed to watch TV except on the weekends, and truthfully, we were all so medicated post-dinner, TV watching was rare. This movie night was thanks to Lily, one of the youngest members of our trauma house. She had bright pink hair and a fire in her heart that sometimes burned people around her. Lily had worked tirelessly for weeks to convince her therapist that it would be a therapeutic experience for us to watch Tangled together instead of doing our nightly meeting. He finally approved it with the condition that we filled out a worksheet comparing the evil stepmother to our disease or our trauma. We filed into the tiny living room; I lay on the floor next to several others, and we laughed and laughed and laughed. It felt like we were children. The mood was festive, a temporary release from the heaviness of our pain.

We were completely deprived of chocolate and desserts except for Thursdays. Sugar was addictive, and even the morning coffee sugar was locked up after women had received their daily ration. Although the weekly promise of chocolate didn't once make me feel anything, being deprived for six days at a time made the other women go crazy as Thursday approached. One day after groups, I was working on something at the kitchen table and a therapist was standing in front of me eating a chewy granola bar with tiny bits of chocolate in it. While he was talking, one fell onto the floor and before I knew what was going on, two grown women dove onto the floor to get it. The winner triumphantly devoured it. I laughed about that for weeks.

As the days leading up to my release drew closer, my three-times-a-week, twenty- minute phone calls were filled with fear from the other side. Noah told me he wasn't quite ready for me to come home. He said he was doing a lot of work on himself. My one call with Summer was one-sided and she told me it didn't feel like I had been gone for very long. My heart sank. It felt like a year to me. My therapist from home told me he thought I should stay another month. I started panicking. It felt like everyone was glad I was gone. I was certain my therapist at treatment had been putting ideas in their heads. I couldn't help but think that she was being given a gift card for each client she re-upped. I told them I was willing to go somewhere else if I needed to, but I would walk myself home if it came to that. I would not stay one hour later than was required.

THEY CALL THEM WARRIORS

Being at treatment was like being buried alive. No matter how many times I ran outside, I could not gulp enough air or harvest enough sun for my skin. The only reason that last proverbial shovelful of earth did not cover my mouth, smothering me, was because of the other women in the house.

Kate, despite being motherly to those around her, was childlike. A beautiful, grown woman, she carried a brightly colored stuffed unicorn around the campus, holding it close and burying her head in it whenever things got intense in group therapy. Her story unfolded during her stay—memories of being molested by her brother and neglected by her mother in the first years of her life. Horrific. Mind numbing. After receiving some trauma therapy, she started rubbing a scar on her arm and remembered spending months in the hospital as a child with severe burns caused by her mother pouring boiling water down her throat and on her skin This was her mother's reaction when Kate spoke the secrets of what her brother had done to her. Her attempt to silence Kate was successful; her daughter lay in the hospital for four months, unable to speak. As if that wasn't enough trauma for two lifetimes, on Kate's ninth birthday her new stepfather brutally raped her. She remembers standing in her bathroom with blood running down her legs and telling her mother what had happened—"Steve stuck his penis in me and ripped me open."—such violent words out of a little girl's mouth. Her mother denied it, shamed her, and defended him. That night when she was blowing out the candles on her birthday cake she didn't smile.

The day before she left treatment, we all gathered around the first birthday cake she'd had since that awful day; the RAs had smuggled in for her on a day that wasn't Thursday. We sang to her as she clutched her stuffed animal and the lights flickered on her bright face. I stared in disbelief. I didn't understand why she wasn't dead. I didn't know why she wasn't a drug addict or a whore. Somehow Kate had clawed her way forward. Fueled by her past, she mothers her three children, pouring out more love in one day than she received in her whole childhood.

Before she left to return home, Kate participated in a psychodrama that lasted for hours. She acted out her story, piece by excruciating piece, and slowly took control of it. The women listened in shock and deep empathy as they too felt many of those feelings from their own stories. I sat and watched them, frozen and terrified. We all chanted to her at parts: "You did nothing wrong!" "Push her out!" We wanted to rescue her. I wanted to hold her, to mother her. My heart ached. At the end, as Sia's "Alive" played over the speakers, we all sat in a circle, hand-in-hand, breathing, crying, smiling, hurting. It was a birth. Kate said it helped to heal her. I felt like it scratched at my already raw skin and made me bleed again.

I still keep in touch with Kate. She is still crawling forward, and I am still in awe of her.

Taylor was my roommate. She was young, and her beauty drew me in from the moment I laid eyes on her. Her long black hair hung down her back in two braids nearly every day. Her face was almost always covered in a smile, but she was going through hell. Taylor had just come from sober living where she had been clean for a year. Every day since she had stopped drinking, old memories that she had drowned for a decade made their way to her mind and her body, resurfacing, unwelcome. Vivid memories attacked her body, and she would be in agony for hours, feeling like she was being raped again. She carried around a pillowcase of rice that she would warm and hold to her belly.

Taylor was wonderful to be around and had a hilarious sense of humor, but it became a rhythm of our day that she would come in and out of reliving horrific experiences. She shared snippets with me as they surfaced in her mind. When these secrets left her lips, it was like dredging up bodies from a bottomless pit of mud. Taylor remembered her father selling her for sex as a small girl. She has vivid memories of being potty trained and seeing her diaper soaked in blood. Of being drugged and locked in a car trunk. At a painfully young age, Taylor started drinking and doing drugs to cover the unbearable. When she was just into her twenties she got pulled over for a DUI and went to jail. After finally becoming sober, she decided to stay sober. Piece by piece, day by day, she pulled off the protective film that had covered her. It burned, it made her bleed, but she did it bravely. I loved her. She scared me. I would watch her throw ice at a tree or toss a hula hoop high into the sky, making groaning sounds that I had never heard before, making my mama heart ache to hold her like the child she was never able to be.

I still hear from Taylor from time to time. She is still here on this earth. She is still choosing to stay here.

When I first saw E.G., I was drawn to her like a magnet. She had a delicate face, a shaved head, dark lashes, and brilliant wide eyes. Her tiny body was hidden by clothes that were a little too big, and she sat in a way that drew attention away from her body. The moment she spoke she blew away any preconceived ideas I had about her. She was a force. She was fiercely protective, kind, but not soft. With a past marked with trauma, she was also struggling to come out of an almost yearlong battle of crippling bipolar depression.

E.G. was an artist and a fellow photographer who focused on the beauty of folds of skin after weight-loss surgery. She was the first person I had ever met with bipolar disorder, and I clung to her. I wasn't alone! We would sit face to face sometimes, and our eyes would connect. Me too. Me too. Me too. My last meal before leaving treatment, I tearfully looked at E.G. from across the table and said, "If the only reason I came here was to meet you, it was worth it." And I meant it.

E.G. and I talk all the time. We check in with a simple, "You stable?" weekly. She forces me to call my doctor when I need it, and I do the same for her. I love her. I need her. E.G. is brilliant; she is a gift this world needs. She doesn't always see that, but I do. And in turn, she sees my brilliance when I can't, and she passionately tells me that I am not a mistake. Life will always be a series of swings for us. We laugh at the funny stuff and hold space for the scary stuff. We remind each other that seasons will end.

Alexis was an Ivy League college student who suffered a breakdown at school after being raped at a party after drinking for her first time.

It was painful to watch her work through the guilt and shame during groups. She was usually pretty hyper and happy, but we all knew she was hurting. Like me, she had a hard time feeling like she deserved to take up space there in that house. The first weeks I just observed her for the most part, but by the second half of my stay we became inseparable. We laughed together, over anything and everything. It felt so strange to laugh so much. I promised her I would send her chocolate-filled tampons in the mail after I left, since we weren't allowed any dessert and she was a chocoholic. The first moment I was alone with my phone after I got out, I searched the internet in vain for chocolate tampons.

I love how complex Alexis is. Even though it is tempting to label her, she can't be put into a category or a box. She's brilliant, graduating college early, even after missing a semester for treatment, but even more impressive is that she paused her life to do the hard work of therapy and treatment at such a young age, when she could have buried her pain with parties and boys. She's goofy, but she's also wise beyond her years. I keep in touch with her; we send funny memes back and forth, she swoons over pictures of my daughter, and we share the hard stuff. I look at her, a decade younger than me, full of life and hope, and I wish I had done hard, intentional work earlier in my life. I know she's not through it, but she certainly has risen time and again, proving that she cannot be silenced.

Elizabeth was the first girl I met in the house. She had cascading brown curls that she kept tucked under a worn, knit hat. She was the baby of our house, and she had many women who mothered her. Elizabeth suffered a childhood of sexual abuse and struggled with self-harm and drugs. She had a beloved cat back home that she talked about incessantly. She carried a stuffed animal cat and talked to it, sometimes even having it speak for her in our groups. One evening Elizabeth got the call that her cat back home had suddenly died. I have never heard such wailing as she fell to the ground. I can't imagine it would sound any different if she lost a child from her own body. Her heart was broken, and the little stability in her life was yanked out from under her.

Elizabeth is doing well now. She has a new cat and a paw tattoo of her old friend on her forearm. I'm so glad she went to treatment. Her heart was beginning to callous, and I think that somehow being in that house, surrounded by nurturers, preserved her beautiful, tender heart.

There was Danielle, who I felt was a kindred spirit. She was a young, alluring bohemian who loved working on puzzles with me. Having grown up in complicated situation of sexual abuse in her home, she was struggling with shame, sex and love addiction, and self-harm. Since treatment, Danielle has become a mother. She's sent me pictures of herself cradling her tiny daughter, and although I know that her journey will not be easy, I have no doubt that she will work tirelessly to protect her. That baby girl is lucky.

Carly was my roommate the last week I was at treatment. She was the most intense person I had ever been with. She was a CrossFit athlete, and her knuckles were always white from anxiety. She had survived a horrific rape while running in college. This came on top of a lifetime of trauma, heartache, and abuse. She suffered debilitating panic attacks that we learned to help her through. Carly didn't like to sit in the pain, and it was hard to watch her try to shake it off. I didn't know her very long, but I know that today she is still fighting to sit in the pain, not numbing it with exercise, alcohol, or disordered eating. A newlywed, she has a sweet husband and a dog she adores. She is simultaneously creating her own beautiful life of memories and giving weight to the past.

There were a dozen other women there with whom I shared that strange time in my life and whom I now love. I stand in amazement, thinking of each precious one, *I can't believe she's still here. I can't believe she didn't die. I can't believe her body can produce laughter.*

They call them warriors. I don't. A warrior is someone who fights, but these women did more than that—they chose to live. There is no name for that. It is holy. Because choosing to really live instead of curling up in the earth to die is the bravest thing I know.

LEAVING

I woke up at three in the morning, my body feeling like it does when a roller coaster takes that first drop, a combination of nauseated and excited. After what seemed like six months, but was actually one, the day finally came that I would go home. I tiptoed in the dark, down the stairs, to the RA on shift, waking her from a light nap in her chair. I asked her to go through my confiscated items that had been kept in the basement. I knew I had to sign off on them before I could pack them and before I could go home. She returned with a black garbage bag in which I found the floral dresses that had faded from my memory, a book that had a cutting scene in it, and the beer shampoo my mother had sent. Several of my friends had found items missing from their things when they checked out, but everything of mine was there, including a now broken bottle of expensive face oil that coated the bottom; the last thing of value they would take from me there. I drew a deep breath and let out a sigh of resignation, crept back up to bed, and lay there tossing and turning, watching the red numbers of the clock edge towards my release.

At last the house started waking up. I got dressed and ready in seconds. My things were already packed by the front door and my drawers were emptied of letters, puzzles, and ugly pants. I compulsively combed my hair to pass the time.

Noah planned to come in the afternoon for my fourth session with my therapist. Remembering how I had been forgotten at the airport when I arrived, I asked the RAs repeatedly if everything on their end was ready so that I could leave immediately after my session. I didn't want to stay a moment longer than I had to. I went through the morning groups and, as always, the anger inside me felt like it would consume me. I closed my eyes and imagined my homecoming in detail: being held in Noah's arms, touching my children's faces, glowing with health. My mask was shined, and my smile was practiced. I was resolved to return to my family soft and pleasant. It felt like I wasn't even the same person anymore. But I was changed by anger, not by therapy.

After one last lunch of microwavable macaroni (which I had grown to love and had hidden behind the frozen vegetables in the freezer that week), I paced up and down the driveway, my eyes scanning the horizon for the telltale dirt cloud of a car coming up the long road. At last I saw it and started running across a field towards the car, as if in a slow-motion movie. I jumped into Noah's arms, sobbing and holding him so tightly I thought our bodies would merge. Time stood still. As I drew back, our eyes found one another. He had changed. He was a stranger, thin from compulsively exercising while I was gone, his mustache too long and hanging over his lip. He had no one to tell him it looked ridiculous.

In therapy, I sat in the dark corner as Noah and my therapist talked about me as though I wasn't there. They were discussing the possibility of me staying another month. I let the words slip over me like a waterfall and tried to push my resentment down. When it was obvious they could not make me stay, we talked about me going to a hospital outpatient program when I returned home. I finally agreed to think about it.

I have to prove I am okay. I must make them believe I'm okay.

I had to get in the facility's van one last time to go to Piney to be examined and discharged. Noah was to meet me there, but it was painful to leave him so soon. Through the whole drive, I felt that something bad was about to happen. Feelings of being trapped made me gasp for breath and scratch at my arms. The tightrope of being okay was so thin, and I gritted my teeth to walk it. In my backpack was a binder full of coping mechanisms, detailed schedules, and self-care lists: do yoga, eat healthy, go for walks, make space to think, take your meds.

Once at Piney, I waited in a chair next to the blood pressure machine and watched a woman walk through the halls, wet with detox sweat. A man was yelling from his room, reminding me of the first day I was there. I closed my eyes. *I'm almost free. I'm almost free.* When everything was cleared for me, the nurse told me she just had to give me my medications to take home. I waited. I waited longer. They were whispering and making calls, searching every cabinet.

"It seems we have lost your medications," a man told me. "We're looking everywhere and calling the nurse who had them last, but she's not picking up."

I wanted to run, but I couldn't. Through a small window I could see Noah sitting in the car he had rented. I just wanted him to come hold my hand. This was happening. Of course it was happening. Those meds were the lifeline, the starring role in my stability. What would happen to me if they couldn't find them? Would I have to stay another night? Would I descend into darkness again?

They looked for more than an hour. I sat silently, tears and snot sliding down my face. As I rocked back and forth, new clients were sticking their heads out of their rooms to take a peek at the girl who was probably just being admitted. The staff came to me empty-handed and said they would send me home with prescriptions, but a few of them were rare and probably wouldn't be able to be filled immediately.

I was trying to suppress my hysteria as a gruff, wiry man, whom I had seen with the male clients, loaded me into Noah's car. He told me to calm down and slammed the door in my face. At least I was free.

Seconds down the road, all the emotions that I had been trying to stifle burst out of me. I screamed all the things I had not been able to say in the brief monitored conversations over the past few weeks: my loneliness, the stories heaped onto me through group therapy, the lies. My fingernails dug into my forearms, and I banged my head against the window. Realizing that Noah was now terrified and wanted to take me back there, I quieted down and apologized. I sat there, numb, furious with myself for already showing him I wasn't okay. The veil was so thin! As we drove to Nashville, to our hotel for the night, Noah timidly reached for my hand. I tried to tell him everything, but the words stumbled out awkwardly. He nodded, but I knew he wasn't really understanding.

My first act as a free woman was to walk into Walgreens and buy a mustache trimmer. The sheer variety of colors and things overwhelmed me. As I checked out, I wanted to look the cashier in the face and tell her I had just escaped.

At the hotel I immediately shaved my legs and arm pits, which I hadn't done during my entire stay. The only razors available had one blade and would leave bloody marks all over the legs of whoever tried to use them. As I put on my floral dress, we got a phone call that they found my meds in a nurse's car; she had forgotten to bring them to Piney. A staff member made the hour-long drive to bring them to us. I was hungry, so we waited in a burger joint, where I ate french fries with cheese. It felt so luxurious. Finally, my bag of meds was placed in my hands with a mild "Sorry." It figures, I thought. My stay at the treatment center started with them forgetting to pick me up and ended with them forgetting my meds, and they didn't care about either mistake.

Later that evening, Noah and I walked to dinner to a fancy place where I ate fresh vegetables and pasta with my knees shaking under the edge of the white tablecloth. I looked around at the bustling room. It had only been a month—not a long time to most people—but it was the longest month away from normalcy you could imagine. I felt like a new visitor to earth as I watched trays of beautifully plated, delicious-smelling food come out of the kitchen. People around me were casually laughing and clinking their glasses as if they didn't know what pain was. I thought about my sisters back at the treatment center. I knew they were gathered around the table giggling over highs and lows. My seat was probably already filled.

That night I fell asleep an hour after Noah. His arms were wrapped around my body, and I cherished the rising and falling of his breath. There was still some intimacy between us after all. I resolved to do better the next day. I would be strong and happy for my return to my children.

HOME

My first morning out of treatment, I woke up in the dark of the
hotel at five o'clock and headed to the bathroom, where I sat on the
floor to journal while Noah slept. I was despondent about my freak-out
the day before over the loss of my meds. I would be seeing my babies
later that day, and I was determined to be my whole and healed self. I
had to put my mask back on and keep it on.

When Noah woke up, we decided to walk a mile to have breakfast
in the city. I had been fantasizing about a latte for a month, and I was
finally going to have one in my hands. The walk was treacherous for
me. Homeless men approached us several times, and I buried my face in
Noah's arm, shaking like a leaf. At one point our GPS directed us to take
a walking bridge that went above part of the city. As we approached,
I panicked as I looked at the asphalt fifty feet below. I saw flashes of
myself jumping over the side, and I backed away in fear. I could not
make myself walk over it. My attempt to act normally was faltering,
and I thought that Noah could see the widening crack in my facade. We
took the long way around to the restaurant, and I luxuriated in the smell
and taste of flaky biscuits and a hot latte with a foamy heart on top. I
drank the latte slowly, warming with each gulp, eyes closed in praise.

The drive home through the twisting mountain roads felt like a journey through an active battlefield. Every stop, turn, and swerve had me gasping and bracing. My heart was thumping the whole time. These were all signs of PTSD. It felt like we would never arrive home to safety.

When we pulled into our driveway, I burst out of my seat to see my babies. Barclay, who is not one to show much emotion, ran into my arms and started crying. He clung to me, and I held him close and inhaled the top of his head. I had not heard his precious voice in more than a month. Sullivan kept looking at me, curious and hesitant. A few minutes later he announced, "It's like how it used to be, Mama." His eyes were bright, and every thought of him being tied up somewhere by a demon disappeared. I woke a sweaty Lucy Miller up from her nap. She stared at me with bleary eyes as if she could not quite place me. A few minutes later she was snuggling in my lap.

My mom was there, too, and looked into my eyes, searching the soul of her girl who had been missing for so long. I held my eyes open as wide and sparkly as they could get and I think she believed I was back. I think I believed it. Mama gave me such an amazing gift that day. She had taught Sullivan to read while I was gone, and we sat on our porch steps as he sounded out the words of a little book he was clutching. He was so proud. I was so relieved. Between my deep depression and my stays in the hospitals around the time he started kindergarten, I had worked on reading with him only once. I felt odd, like a visitor in my own home.

Once the kids were in bed, I sat awkwardly on the couch facing Noah. "I'm doing a seven-hour bike ride tomorrow. I've arranged childcare, so you don't have to worry about that," Noah said, rigidly.

I was stunned and horrified and devastated, all at once. He held fast against my pleading. "I'm learning to take care of myself. I need this," he said.

The vision I had of my first day home with my family was blotted out. Heat filled my body, and I started pleading with him to stay with me. His face was blank. I wanted to hurt myself and grabbed a marker, drawing where I wanted to cut. Somehow I countered that with what I had been taught to do at treatment: I filled a bucket with ice water and submerged my head under it for thirty seconds. But that didn't make me feel better, and I took a knife out of the drawer and tried to cut my arms. Noah grabbed it away in disgust. I got my hands on a container of oatmeal, threw it all over the kitchen, and fell on my knees sobbing.

"Just love me. Please, just love me," I wailed. Nothing.

I was covered in oatmeal, and my hair was dripping wet. I looked ridiculous.

That night I fell into bed ashamed and scared, but the new morning brought new hope. The children were gone, and I was alone for the first time in months. I tried to push away the pain I had felt the night before. I went to the store and bought yellow tulips I opened all our doors and let the warm spring air fill our home and my lungs. I played Sia's "Bird Set Free" and danced and danced. I danced for two hours, raising my arms every time she sang the chorus, "I don't want to die, I don't want to die!"

And I didn't.

DEATH AND DECAY

I stared out my bedroom window at the tall, majestic trees on my street. A wail rose from my throat, and tears filled my eyes. These trees would grow too big for this space and would one day die. All the trees would, and no one was planting new ones. My stomach ached. One day this whole street would be bare.

The finality of life was hard to bear post-treatment. I became obsessed with trees falling on me. If one looked old or unsteady, I would listen at its trunk for any creaks or groans before walking under it. Seeing a fallen tree filled me with dread. Everything was dying.

During my free time I walked aimlessly by the river and came home with armloads of trash. I researched and groaned as I learned what happens to all our garbage. The decay of the earth was paralyzing. I texted friends about it late at night. I was concerned that the additional weight from the mountains of trash would cause the earth to move away from the sun, killing us all. No one sensed the severity of the situation but me.

I stared at the elderly with disbelief. How could they function, knowing their life was hastening to an end? My beloved Aunt Lucy died that spring, and I couldn't shake the thought of what happened to her physical body—the absence of breath, the life draining out of her like water out of a bathtub. As I stood on the grave of my six-year-old cousin and watched my ninety-year-old aunt being lowered into the ground, the realization that I almost died myself overtook me. I looked around, wondering if anyone else was thinking the same thing. I imagined my children peering down into my grave, their faces twisted with confusion and grief. It was almost me.

That spring, our shaggy gray rabbit also died. We found him, hard as a rock, after a rainstorm and buried him in the yard. The children gathered stones and flowers to lay on top of the grave. As the weeks ticked by, I often wondered what our rabbit looked like under the earth. Months later, the children and I decided to dig him up to see what had happened. We gingerly laid out his white bones, so tiny and light. There were sacred whispers as we looked over each and every one. Seeing them white and clean was miraculous to me. It comforted me.

I walked through the graveyard near my house. I could see through the dirt, through the coffins, piles and piles of bones. I kept my morbid thoughts to myself.

Even so, death and decay surrounded me everywhere I looked: global warming, plastic in the bellies of fish, breathing bodies of souls already lost rotting in nursing homes, methane gas, animal carcasses, waste, plastic toys from China piled higher than Mount Everest, and big beautiful trees that cannot live forever.

IT WAS JUST LEMONADE

I felt like I was failing at everything when I came home from treatment. Everything was hard. I longed for wholeness and the healing of our family. I longed to be that nightgown mom I had always wanted to be. After talking to Amy about it, she helped me come up with one small goal for the week: to give my kids a snack every day after school.

I went to the store to find something; it was my only plan for the day. I walked the aisles and became overwhelmed and jittery. When I saw the lemonade I went straight to it. I picked it up and held it in my hands. It was cold and wet. I closed my eyes and was transported to my kitchen, where I saw myself in a floral apron, cheeks flushed, tendrils of hair framing my face, laughing and serving lemonade to my children as we talked about their day. My bond with them strengthened.

I put the bottle in my empty cart and checked out with only one item. At home I waited by the door for them to come so I could surprise them. I tied my apron and smoothed it down, the lemonade tucked safely in our fridge. When they came bounding in, I excitedly told them what I had for them. They cheered! I poured them all big glasses and sat across from them as they chatted away. *I did it! I did it!* I told myself. It was happening; I was living my dream.

I went upstairs to get something and came back down to see that the whole bottle was empty. They had snuck an extra glass each as soon as I left the room. I fell on my knees, put my forehead to the floor, and wailed, then I got up and screamed at my children. As terrible words poured out, their little faces went white. As if I were watching myself from across the room, I got scared too. I ran upstairs, locked myself in the bathroom, and texted Noah to come home. The beautiful picture I had created in my mind was a fake. Flooded with shame, I grabbed a knife and cut my arms. My vision blurred, and all I saw was red. I heard Noah downstairs consoling the kids, once again cleaning up the mess I had made. First he took care of them, then he took care of me. I knew that I was the problem, that I was the poison. That I would never be okay.

I made dinner, but I didn't cook in my apron. As I sat down at the table, my eyes drawn to my lap, a small drop of blood ran down my arm and plopped on the floor.

It was just lemonade.

THERAPY

When I left treatment, I was emotionally malnourished. I returned to normal life armed just with a notebook of DBT skills and a list of items to keep in a bag for emergencies. The first day home I started filling my brown leather purse with lotion, soft molding clay, fidget toys, gum, word searches, and Icy Hot pain-relieving cream. I gripped that bag as though it held my salvation. Despite my best efforts, it was painfully obvious in the first week that the contents of my bag were not a substitute for intensive therapy. As hard as it was for me to admit, staying at home doing normal things was out of the question. I longed for open-aired freedom, but I still needed to be cared for. I followed the advice of my therapist at treatment and enrolled myself into an intensive outpatient program at the local hospital—the same hospital that had the women's psych unit I had been admitted to twice.

The program was small and only for women, but still it scared me. Flashes of the treatment center filled my mind, but I decided to stay because I knew I only had to go three mornings a week and could go home after lunch.

I arrived with my bag of tricks and a backpack of coloring books and crocheting. I would not sit idle at that terrible place like I had before. The class was sweet. I was relieved to again be around other people who weren't okay. We did a daily check-in that was worth everything. I would fill out a page, answering simple questions and rating my suicidal ideations. It was grounding. I listened to the DBT skills being taught while focusing on distracting my fingers from making my skin bleed. The best part of the day was when we all got a voucher to go to the cafeteria and have lunch together. I had dignity there and felt the power of not being alone.

Throughout this time, I was plagued with recurring visions that felt like they had happened to me. I could see it clearly: wallpaper, a body falling in slow motion body, sounds. An image of my daughter being thrown over our stair railing replayed in my mind hundreds of times a day. Sometimes it was her, sometimes it was me. They woke me up during the night and caused me to squeeze my eyes closed in terror while driving down the road.

I also had obsessions of Lucy drowning. The dream I had when I was in treatment, of her floating in the pool, haunted me, and whenever I closed my eyes I could see her lifeless body floating with parted lips, and wide, vacant eyes. I found myself waking several times a night to check the bathtubs and toilets for her body. The things I was capable of doing and thinking when I was insane felt real. My mom had a pool in her backyard, and when she would watch her I could barely stand it, calling several times an hour to check on Lucy.

When things felt completely out of hand and critical, I decided to try EMDR—eye movement desensitization and reprocessing—therapy. All I knew about it was that it was used to treat soldiers with PTSD. I wasn't a combat veteran, and I felt unworthy walking into the therapist's office. But I went anyway, and after several sessions of just chatting, she decided that I was stable enough to do EMDR. I giggled and felt clumsy as she placed vibrating balls in each of my hands and walked me through the process. We started with a disturbing memory, which I described to her, after which I let my mind go wherever it wanted while the balls buzzed back and forth until she stopped me. Then I described whatever I saw next. Sometimes it was related, but oftentimes it was spaghetti or a dog with a hat on. And that seemed to be the gist of it. The procedure was simple and straightforward, the opposite of the emotionally charged psychodramas. Several times I almost walked out, it seemed so pointless, but after just a few sessions, my recurring visions ceased and I could sleep at last.

DEATH AND RESURRECTION

Spring brought relief from the suicidal thoughts, but it also split me open and turned me inside out, exposing all my nerves. I was raw, and even the gentlest breeze made me recoil violently.

In previous years, spring awoke my cold skin with a gentle brush and a whisper of hope. I would walk my children up and down our street oohing and aahing at the blossoms, shaking the cherry trees so that they snowed pink all around us. We called them love trees. But this year, when the earth was budding and growing and living, I was rotting and shrinking and dying.

Every interaction with Noah was painful. The more I needed him, the more he withdrew. He exercised compulsively, often leaving me for hours. He preached self-care to me and pushed me away when I asked him to be present. He fell asleep early and slept till he had to go to work. He was connecting with anyone and everyone but me. He was seeing a therapist and finding himself, but he was the least him I had ever known. One night after the kids were in bed, I asked him to tell me if he saw just one small thing of beauty in me. I was starving for it.

"No," he replied through tight lips.

I gave him all the power. I gave him my heart, ripping it from my chest and placing it in his hands. But he didn't want it.

The more I needed him, the more he literally went away. No matter how hard I tried, I could not empty myself of my need. I was obsessed with making him feel close to me again. I wrote in my journal:

I've never felt more alone, more burdensome, more worthless in my life. It was a slow funeral march at the end of a long battle.

Step, step, step.

Will my whole life be a weary lament?

It feels like it.

I can barely picture myself free anymore.

Picture myself without arms bleeding and scratched.

Maybe I want to bleed.

Maybe I want to die.

When I think of that spring, I think about bloody cardigans. I would wear them to cover the rows of cuts up and down my arms, even when it was hot outside. One day, when I had lost the will to care, I stopped covering my arms, curious what others would say. I didn't wound myself because I wanted attention, I did it to breathe. Every time Noah saw what I had done, he hated me more. Once, he walked into the house to find drops of blood leading up to the second floor. He grew icy and left the house. He made me feel like I would hurt the children, like I was something to run away from. No one acknowledged the cuts except for my mother.

I found myself standing inside a closet cutting myself while the kids played outside or sneaking scissors into a bathroom at a gathering with friends. I did it because each cut felt like a gulp of fresh air. I did it because a knife in my hand gave me control when I felt helpless.

One morning in late spring, when the kids were miraculously occupying themselves with crafts in the dining room, I had a renewed burst of resolve. I walked past the mountain of bills on our table and decided to call our Christian cost sharing healthcare company to verify that they did not, indeed, cover my mental health bills. A kind-sounding man named Paul answered. When I told him what I was calling about, he confirmed that they do not cover mental health (a true lack of Christian care) and started asking questions about the details of my case. I thought maybe he had a payment option for me if my case was bad enough; maybe he wanted to make sure I wasn't "just a depressed housewife." I proceed to walk him through some of the worst of my experiences, including my suicidal and homicidal thoughts, always referring to them in the past tense.

He kept pressing. "Mrs. George, are you sure you don't want to have a brain scan? Maybe if you do they'll find a brain tumor, and then we can cover this for you."

This man actually wanted me to have a brain tumor. He wanted me to want to have a brain tumor so I could get my bills covered. So I would fit in their box.

I tried to end the conversation, and he asked if he could pray for me. I reluctantly agreed and hung up as soon as he was finished. As I went to the kids and started to help them cut paper, I heard a knock at our door. Scissors in hand, I answered and saw two police officers with their hands on their guns.

"Drop the scissors on the ground!" they shouted.

I dropped them.

"We have received a report that you want to hurt your children, and we need to search the house."

I tried to explain. I tried to tell them how those thoughts were far behind me and how the man who called actually wanted me to have a brain tumor. Obediently, I stepped to the side as they searched my house and questioned my kids. Any sense of steadiness I had felt that morning dissipated. Fortunately, they didn't stay long and left with an apologetic tinge to their words. The children asked me why they had come, and I told them they were checking on everyone in the neighborhood.

As the birds chirped and the sun grew hot, my will to live waned. I had done everything anyone had asked of me: therapy, walks, prayer, healing prayer, hospitals, pills, rehab. And I felt completely abandoned.

A friend sent me an album on iTunes, and I happened upon a song that spoke the exact words of my wounded heart— "The Rain Keeps Falling" by Andrew Peterson. I put my earphones in and pressed play. I wasn't alone. His words gripped me. My favorite lyrics from the song are:

My daughter and I put the seeds in the dirt
And every day now we've been watching the earth
For a sign that this death will give way to a birth
And the rain keeps falling...

I fantasized about planting seeds with my daughter and waiting for the growth. Oh, the wait was agony. I wanted the fruit, the bloom, right then.

That Easter Sunday, I played violin for our church service. Playing on that day made me feel like I was standing on holy ground, so I kicked off my shoes under my long skirt. The resurrection had always been living and breathing for me, bursting with hope. That year I swayed while I played. Empty. Numb from longing for a savior to come for me. Everyone was celebrating the resurrection, and I couldn't stop looking at the tomb.

PLEASE HELP ME

I am trying so hard to stay alive. It feels like trudging through deep mud. Even the eyes of my children can't bring me back. LM reached for me in her sleep during a dream and that helped, but almost nothing else. I am most assuredly a burden. My patience is nonexistent and I am harming young spirits with my cruelty. I just don't want to be here anymore.

I wrote this in my journal just a few days before admitting myself to the psych ward for the fourth time.

One April night, after the kids were in bed and Noah was snoring, my loneliness became unbearable. I stood in my bedroom, watching Noah's chest rise and fall with a steady breath. The life in him taunted me. I wanted to be as alive as he was. I imagined taking all my pills and climbing into bed and curling around his body. I would grow cold next to him. I reached for the pill bottles and emptied them out. The contents spilled out of my hands and onto the floor. The sound startled me, but Noah continued to snore.

"Help me! Please help me!" I cried out to my sleeping husband.

I felt powerless to keep death at bay for another minute. Noah rolled over, looked at me with those pills in my hands, and with a blank face said, "Call 911." And he rolled over and went back to sleep.

By some power greater than my own, I managed to put all the pills back and proceeded to fill my suitcase with a puzzle, some slippers, my favorite dress, and my journal. Either I was going to die that night or I was going to the hospital in the morning.

Somehow I managed to drift off to sleep, and when I awoke in the morning, I helped get my children off to school. I did not hug them goodbye. I told Noah I wouldn't be back, that I was going to admit myself that day. I didn't expect him to say anything. Even if he was disappointed in me, it could not be more than I was in myself. Almost matter-of-factly, I loaded my suitcase into the car and drove off to the hospital.

I decided to go to my outpatient class, but first I marched to the nurses station, pulled up the sleeves of my cardigan, and showed the woman on duty my bloody arms.

"I don't want to live anymore," I said with no inflection or emotion. She brought in the same psychiatrist who had given me that fateful prescription months earlier. My mask made them cock their heads to the side while they examined me, wondering if I was serious. As they silently questioned me, my resolve started to waver.

"Do you think maybe I just need to go to a hotel and get away from my family for a few days?"

A collective "no" resounded.

I attended the class for two hours while they worked on getting me admitted. Because I was in the program, I could bypass the ER admission, which would save me thousands of dollars and hours of waiting. I checked off level ten out of ten for suicidal thoughts on my daily check-in. I crocheted furiously as the instructor discussed coping skills. A large pair of blue scissors across the room caught my eye. The patches of uncut flesh on my legs and arms teased me. During our first break, I slipped the scissors up the sleeve of my sweater and went to the bathroom, where I savagely cut every clean space I could see. I threw the scissors away, pushing them to the bottom of the trash can, under the mound of paper towels. I returned to class with blood dripping down my thighs, seeping into my long black skirt. No one noticed. Twenty minutes later, I returned to the bathroom and retrieved the scissors from the trash can. I did not wash them. Again I cut, frightened that it wasn't enough and that maybe the unit would think I was lying, that they wouldn't believe my pain. Then I carefully washed the scissors and took them back to class in my sleeve.

At last a bed was available, and I left class abruptly to claim it. As the nurse walked me to the unit that I was so familiar with, my phone dinged with an email from my mom. Just the few lines that appeared on my home screen filled me with dread. I felt sick. I had disappointed her. I shut down my phone, handed it over, and walked in. All of the nurses knew my name. I let them guide me through the process I knew so well: blood pressure, temperature, strip search. The nurse didn't even flinch when she saw my wounds. I should have done more, I thought to myself. I was desperate that she wouldn't know how badly I hurt.

That night I lay in my stiff hospital bed, and it felt like I had never felt the tender touch of humanity, like my mother had birthed me and never held me to her breast. My feet tangled in the scratchy sheet as I writhed and arched my back.

"Where are you, God?" I cried out into my small room. "Where did you go? Why did you abandon me? Why won't you save me? Why aren't you healing me? I've done everything anyone has asked of me! Am I not worthy of love? Save me or kill me! Give me breast cancer. Let a truck run over me. Why, why, why have you forsaken me?" Over and over and over I screamed it. I didn't care who heard me.

Christ on the cross, crying out the same things, came to my mind, and I knew that He was there. Regardless of my feelings, I knew that He was there. I didn't know why He didn't save me, but I did know that He was familiar with this loneliness, with this grief.

I had never felt isolation like that. I flashed back to myself as a little girl under the bed, aching for someone to see me. That night in the hospital, it felt like the end.

I AM BRAVE

At six o'clock I woke up to the soft glow of the hall light illuminating the nurse coming in for the early morning blood pressure check I had grown accustomed to. My belly burned; sleep had been a sweet relief from the all-consuming hopelessness I was feeling, and waking from it was jarring. I got out of bed and looked at the morning questionnaire I had to fill out before breakfast.

What is your goal for today?

"To be alive," I wrote.

After breakfast I returned to my bed, passing the phone in the hall and choosing not to call anyone. The chaplain came to my room to invite me to the morning devotional, and I coldly said, "No."

I was disgusted with myself. I didn't recognize the woman I was. It was as if I had died.

I didn't go to any groups that day. I didn't eat dinner. I slept hard, almost like I was drugged, but none of my meds had changed. Memories of the women in all the hospitals and in treatment who slept and didn't participate in groups flooded my mind. I had hated those women. I hated myself. I woke up for evening snack, stumbling into the kitchen in my hospital gown. I had not bothered to put my clothes on. I sat down, heavy in my chair, and glanced around the room. I was repulsed. There was no beauty in any of us.

That evening at group, we went around with our nightly paper, taking turns answering questions like "Did you meet your goal?" At the bottom it said, "Write an affirmation about yourself."

I could not see an ounce of worth in my lumpy, empty body. I finally scratched, "I am brave" on mine. I was grotesque, but I was brave.

From across the room, a woman read off her affirmation in a country twang, "Well, I guess I never did cheat on my second husband." I couldn't even laugh. Before bed I jotted down her comment in my journal so I could laugh about it later.

That night I slept nineteen hours without the use of any drugs. It hurt to be awake.

The next day was visitation day. I had not communicated with my family, and I didn't even know if any of them wanted to see me. Summer showed up for a thirty-minute visit. I felt embarrassed that she had come—unworthy of her time. As she left, two family members that I wasn't expecting to see came in and sat near me in my room. I ached for their love. I imagined that they would cover me with words of hope.

"We've come to cast out a demon from you. It's obvious you don't want to be better. You're doing this for attention. We believe you've invited this demon into you because you watch apocalyptic movies."

The barrage of ugly words suffocated me. I slumped against the wall and let my wounded forearms fall open. One of them rubbed the cuts. They were desperate. They had no control over my healing, and they were hurting too.

"You are doing this on purpose. You like being like this. You just want attention."

As if a steady water were rising around my head, I started panicking.

Finally they ended with, "Now, we would like to pray this demon out in the name of Jesus."

I blinked.

"No," I said.

Blink. Blink.

"I believe I have Christ inside of me, so I don't believe that a demon can live there."

It came out of my mouth before I could form it in my mind.

Two stunned faces looked back at me.

They stammered on, tears filling their eyes as they told me they still thought demons could be surrounding me and proceeded to pray without my consent. I kept my eyes opened and on the wall in front of me. *I just need love.*

After I had walked them to the door the nurse asked, "How was your visit, honey?"

"Well, they tried to cast a demon out of me."

I returned to my room in shock. Their words echoed in the small space, and I could not even begin to understand how anyone could think I was doing this for attention. *Don't they know how awful it is to feel like I do? To be in this place?* The loneliness, the suffocating feeling I always carried, weighed heavy. I had given up on myself, and so had everyone else.

That evening the same nurse gave me my meds with a little wink, "These are good for demons."

Once again, before bed that night, I scratched on my paper, "I am brave."

I did not believe it, but I wrote it anyway.

The next day I finally called Noah, and he told me he was thinking of getting an apartment for himself for a few months. He was completely shut down, and our marriage appeared pretty bleak. I could feel his disgust with me across the phone lines. The news of an impending separation didn't sink in; I was numb.

Providentially, the psych ward doctor who had belittled and nearly killed me was on vacation that week, so I saw a PA who was covering for him. During my first meeting with her, she pulled out a large piece of paper, and for over an hour we mapped out a plan. She created a schedule for administering small doses of antipsychotic meds throughout the day in hopes that I could get a handle on the cutting and stop feeling suicidal. She was cheerful and genuine. She believed in me.

When I finally stopped sleeping through everything, I started getting to know the other women. There was a girl who called herself Kitten. She was nineteen, and I overheard her telling her mom on the phone that she thought she could get her own place after being on the psych unit.

"Mom. I've learned life skills. I learned how to brush my own teeth, and I did a load of laundry."

There was Anne, a simple woman, the mental age of a six-year-old, with ink-black hair and bright red cheeks. She rocked a lot and clapped her hands like a child.

Then there was Tina, a woman with breasts bigger than watermelons and a voice deeper than Johnny Cash's. She slept all day and would come out at meal times and sit with her hospital gown open in the back and her naked butt on the cold metal chair. She ate hunched over, rotating each breast, one at a time, to hang between her legs.

Days passed neither quickly nor slowly. Everything felt gray. I didn't feel good, but I started not to feel bad either. I didn't put on my mask this time to get out early, and eventually I was well enough to go. I'm sure there was a woman down in the ER waiting for my bed.

The day they told me I could go home, I ate lunch and packed up my belongings. I felt like I would be back again soon and wondered if I should just stash my things in the laundry room. For the first time in this weary story, I wasn't desperate to get out. What awaited me at home? Disappointment? Trauma? While I waited for my discharge papers to be finalized, I went into the kitchen to join a group of women who were doing music therapy. We sang the lyrics from old, laminated binders with no accompaniment, taking turns picking favorites. Everyone sang off-key.

"Scars to Your Beautiful" was chosen, and eight women sang in broken unison. I mouthed the words and noticed my cheeks were wet. I looked around the room at the worn out, haggard women. I was officially a member of that group.

My papers were ready, and I left them there in that small room. I rolled my suitcase out to the car and drove myself home. It felt like a joke. I cut myself in the first hour. Noah had agreed to have out-of-town guests stay with us that night and the two following. After an evening beside our outdoor fireplace, I went upstairs to go to sleep and heard

Noah talking about his disassociation with me to our guests. I pressed my cheek against the cold window and cut my legs to the rhythm of his voice.

I closed my eyes.

I am brave.

RESCUER

I look into his deep, brown eyes and wonder, *Has he abandoned me? What can I do to make him see me?* Because no matter how I contort my body and spirit, I cannot please him, cannot bring warmth back into his eyes. But who will love him if I don't?

The ache of our own broken families pulses in my belly. I am determined to reclaim our marriage for our children, no matter the pain it brings me.

His propensity to turn his back when I need him to lean in has always been there. Our misfires are magnified by our family dynamics and a chasm of an age gap.

I want rescuing. I want to be cradled and told I am not too much, that I am lovely just as I am. I want someone to counteract the voices screaming from within me. I want a hand reaching out to save me when I am drowning, not a foot standing on my head.

We did have laughter. Always laughter. We had our children and intimate moments in the birth room right before they entered the world. We had adventures around the world and the discovery of new cultures, which filled our hearts. We hosted the loveliest parties and, once in a while at weddings, he would swing me around the dance floor using the three moves he learned the month we got married, and our eyes would lock. Maybe he liked a sliver of me.

He never beat me.

But that isn't enough.

I've sat through hundreds of therapy sessions over a decade and a half, praying that any faint memories of childhood abuse he may have had to endure would surface, explaining his cruelty towards me, his icy resistance to me. Those memories never came. I've cried out for answers, because if there are none, it means that it is all my fault. It means that I am, in fact, impossible to love.

Sometimes I find myself on the floor, leaning against my whirring dishwasher, fists clenched in despair, asking why? Why did I choose someone who echoed my childhood insecurities? Why did I choose someone who turned his back on my beauty and whispered lies about who I was? Why did I choose someone who found connection in everyone but me?

Maybe I didn't choose him; maybe he chose me.

Why don't I run far away, my children in tow? Because deep down I see a glowing, loving heart in him. I see it. I've caught glimpses of it for twenty years, and it is magnificent. I believe in him despite my failed attempts at chipping away at the walls surrounding his heart, his compassion. All I need is to blast out just a tiny chunk from his deep, cold wall. I beat my fists on it and cry, "I want to free you! I want to love you! I want to rescue you!"

REBORN

I want to be reborn.

I dig my nails deep, grasping at the next layer of skin and clawing at it to separate. It hurts. Every ounce of my body hurts as I pull off my flesh. I want to have new skin, pink and smooth. I want to be reborn. I want to be free.

Sometimes in my darkest moments I see a vision of myself, lying down on the earth with a hundred bodies lying on top of me. Their skin melts with mine. These crushing bodies are my mother's secrets, my father's lies, sudden deaths, affairs, children who never came home from the hospital, crumbling marriages, carcasses piled high.

I think of my grandmother Helen, who wasn't allowed to nurse her own babies because she was told "only slaves and animals" did that, and who asked to hold my newborn baby to her bare, ninety-year-old breasts when I was a new mother. I handed him, tiny and innocent, to her, and she held him tightly to her thin nightgown and rocked and rocked. Her sorrow was fresh after all those years. I wanted to tell her how lovely I thought her asking to breastfeed my baby was. The despair of not being able to nurture your own children the way you want to, the way you were created to, is poisonous. It poisoned my father. I still have a taste of it myself.

Lying here on this ground, heavy and tasting like the bitter earth, I feel a resolve to fight. I want to peel and scratch all of this filth away. I want the pain my grandfather felt after the war to end with me so that my children never know it. I want to erase the ache of mothers who lost children centuries ago, so it does not pass on to my children. I want the splintering from my parents' divorce not to seep into their souls.

Why do I push away all of the fake happiness I could conjure up every day, like normal people? Because it's easier to ignore the pile of filth and keep putting a golden cloak of cheer over it than it is to name it, "This is pain, this is hurt."

So I scratch and I pull so I don't suffocate.

I do it for my children in hopes that one day they realize I have only handed them one body to heap onto their backs. Mine. One layer that they must work through and peel aside. So that they can have pink skin too.

REDEEMED

It started with an early morning sunrise on the deserted beach where my family was staying for a week in Costa Rica. My last hospital stay was six months behind me. We all came out of our netted beds, sticky and hot, and made our way to the water's edge. I had Lucy on my hip, and Noah snapped a picture of me facing the horizon. Everything was still and gentle, and wholeness filled me. When I saw the image, I was in awe. I couldn't recognize myself.

I almost died, I thought. And here I am standing on this beach with my family, watching a new day begin.

The contrast of that moment with the previous year was so far reaching. I decided to share the picture with some words on Instagram and hashtagged it #theyearialmostdied.

"What a heavy, dark, clawing-through-mud year it has been for our family," I wrote. "This trip has been true joy for me. I feel so full of light again. I feel so capable of being a mother. I even woke up to see the sunrise today. So unbelievably grateful to still be here."

I felt that I had laid claim to a small plot of land. Taking back something I owned. Redeeming it.

As the leaves started to change and the air grew cool with fall, haunting memories started rushing back. Unwelcome memories. Their intensity was frightening. Still, I celebrated every personal victory, no matter how small. One by one, I laid my claim to them, taking the power back.

I posted this on Instagram next to a picture of me in my favorite twirly dress:

"Today is a victory day! I woke up and put on my pretty dress, brushed my hair extra good and headed off to see my psychiatrist. You see, for months and months and months I would show up (barely being able to make it from week to week) in my pajamas, with my hair dreaded with twigs and leaves and I just didn't think I could live another day. I would cry and cry and my wonderful psychiatrist would promise me that one day I would be healthy and sit in his office in my right mind. Happy and healthy. My mind couldn't even comprehend that, but today I walked into that office, proud as can be and wanting to scream and cry from gratefulness. I am a version of myself I didn't think would ever be possible. A victory indeed. I know that with this disease I will never be "healed" and that there will be other seasons of hard, but today I'm celebrating and making sure I never let it go that long again without help."

On the first anniversary of admitting myself into the first hospital, I felt a looming wave of terror. Memories of being trapped and alone were palpable. But instead of letting them consume me, I focused my energy on gathering books, art supplies, and puzzles to donate to the holding unit. "For the forgotten," I told the nurse who took the five boxes from me in disbelief. I turned my back on that house of horrors and walked away. Redeemed.

As the days grew shorter, the darkness crept in.

I told my story to anyone who would listen to me. I posted it on Instagram, I told the lady at the checkout counter. I uttered the truth. I didn't try to gloss over it.

Day after day, I got messages in return.

"Me too."

"My sister just committed suicide, and I never understood."

"I'm so depressed, but I've finally decided to get help."

It smoothed the scars.

Every day brought new memories and yet more new victories. The act of storytelling was healing wounds no therapist could touch.

"It's Christmas. Exhale. When I was so bad off for so many months and I knew I wouldn't be better in days, weeks or months, I KNEW I would be better by Christmas. Lying alone, states away, I would pretend to be asleep so I could have time to think, and I would imagine Christmas down to the minute details. In hospitals. In my bathroom with my arms bleeding. How it would smell and feel, what music would be playing. Most of all I would imagine the connection I would finally have healed between my family.

My scars are deep and far reaching. I still am having such a hard time with my children (leaps and bounds from last year). It hurts, and then it's so beautiful I cannot catch my breath, and then I feel hopeless and then the hope is so bright I can't see.

I'm here. My life was spared. I have grown in ways I never wanted to, and yet it's already obvious that it was not all in vain.

Christmas will not, cannot, look like it did in all my vivid fantasizing. But my brain is present this year, my heart is full, and I have a precious family. That's enough.

The long-awaited light has come down."

Christmas was not to be redeemed in one fell swoop, but in tiny victories and with a whole lot of mourning. My body hurt, my children reacted to everything with violence, mourning the fact that their mama was stolen from them the previous year.

"Tonight I laid under the tree with my middle one. He is the deepest feeler of my three and has struggled with "mama being sick" the hardest. He cried and thrashed and screamed for more than four hours today and we were all just at a loss of how to help him. When we were laying under the tree he said, 'Mama we did this last year . . . but you were really, really sick.' Tears. Silent tears as he babbled on while we looked at the lights. It hurts so bad."

Every day I would sit in my big armchair and open up Ann Voskamp's advent book. I played Josh Garrels' "The Light Came Down" on repeat, and I wept for light. The darkness, the loneliness, and the helplessness were so near to me again. I wanted the light more than anything.

Christmas Eve came, and I had vivid memories of cutting my arms in the dark kitchen at church before the Christmas Eve service the year before. I wanted to control the narrative of this redemption story, but trauma took control with a flourish.

"I'm still in anguish, my arms are covered in wounds, new and old. There are so many people who are hurting and hungry and beaten. The darkness is so thick. But there are glimmers of hope, of light. Light has been given to us AND it is coming to us."

I posted that before walking into church to play violin at the Christmas Eve service. I scoured the Sunday school rooms for a pair of scissors and hid in the nursery, making marks up and down my arms. It felt like I had lost everything I had worked so hard for. My redemption was not in my control.

Christmas morning came fresh and sacred. A gift.

The new year approached, and I finally felt like I had my footing, like the worst was behind me, littered with tiny red flags. Victories. That's when the Department of Social Services knocked at my door with the sheriff's deputy to question my children. A vindictive two-page report had been filed against our family for neglect. In it were many details that I had written and posted publicly, but some of them were so private, we don't know how anyone else could know. Most of it was outright lies. The case was closed within minutes of meeting with the caseworker in our living room the following week, but the trauma of the accusations reopened deep wounds.

So I started the new year on the floor of my dirty laundry room, unable to wake from the sting of betrayal and the guilt of what I had done to my family. I stopped speaking; I stopped peeling at the grimy filth that covered me. Then I started getting sick. I felt trapped and would wake up gasping for breath. Panic attacks returned with a vengeance. It wasn't until I released my fears and continued putting words to my experiences and telling my story that healing would begin again.

The cycle was continuous: a victory, mourning, redemption, and taking control over helplessness. It was messy. It was unpredictable. It was life giving.

As the winter thawed and spring returned, the sickly feeling of decay overpowered me. The warm breeze touched my skin, and I remembered everything from the year before. My arms ached from wounds that had healed. As I spoke out loud the things that had remained hidden in the darkest corners of my mind, I felt lighter. I joined the animals in shedding my winter heaviness. I bought yellow tulips every time I could.

One warm April day at MerleFest, a bluegrass festival we go to every year, I sat listening to the music and taking in my surroundings. A year before, I had just been released from my final hospital stay. My arms had been bloody, and I couldn't dance.

Noah took a picture of me that day. I was beaming. I wrote these words:

"The months, no, years, leading up to a year ago could be described as a slow crawl on my bleeding knees up a mountain so tall I couldn't see the top. When I got a little higher I would fall and slide, slumping into a heap and almost giving way to the earth. But then I got up and tried again. During Merlefest last year I was bloody and drained of every last ounce of fight, but I had finally reached the top. And the days/weeks/ months following could be described as a shedding. Layer by layer, peeling back filth and hurt and grime. So many layers. I was heavy and crouched over, but pounding on the walls of self to let me free. Working through this year I almost died has set me free. It hurt so bad. It hurt so bad, and many would say reliving it all was bad for me, was bad for my family. But I want to scream from the top of this beautiful mountain that I am free from the weight that year had on my body and spirit.

Now look at that beautiful spirit, that smile that comes from a place deeper than I can name.

She lived."

EPILOGUE

I had just checked into a little cabin in the woods to finish this book, freshly medicated to suppress a recent manic episode. I was barely "allowed" to go. After all, I had spent upwards of forty hours purchasing a vintage apron for nearly everyone I knew and researching antique letter openers for who knows what reason. In the last hours before my rental was ready, my husband cautiously said I could go. I was elated. Several times on the hour-long drive there, I pulled over to jot thoughts down on an old receipt as they came pouring into my head. My heart beat fast as I pull up to the tiny cabin, draped in fairy lights. I was going to finish this book there.

Writing about conquering mental illness while you are, in fact, flat on your ass again, is humbling and confusing. I wanted a clean-cut story: a struggle and a triumph, a mountain scaled, clawing out of a grave, finally seeing the light in the darkness, finding hope. I wanted to type the period at the end of the last sentence and yell, "Done!" Yet, every minute, I am reminded that life is not like that.

At ten o'clock the first night at the cabin, I realized that I had forgotten the very medicine I so desperately needed to keep me from starting this narrative over again. I walked around the small room of the cabin, pacing, writing, and doing a puzzle. I was convincing myself that

I would be okay. After midnight I finally decided I had better go get it. I walked to my car in the dark and drove away. A mile down the road I looked down to find I was topless and realized I had not put on my glasses. I spent the drive bent forward, trying to make out which side of the road to drive on while protecting my bare chest from the breeze coming through the open windows. I drove so slowly, it took more than an hour until I reached my house. While my family slept peacefully upstairs, I broke in and grabbed my pills. Catching a glance of myself in the reflection of a window, I couldn't stop laughing. Before driving back I made a mental note to write an epilogue and include this story.

It doesn't end, friends. This story does not end with a beautiful bow wrapping up the contents of a lifetime of trying to stay alive. I wrote this book with mania running through my veins. I wrote it slumped in a chair. I wrote it sobbing, naked, on the floor. I scratched it onto bits of paper and spoke it into my phone. I want to control my story. I want to contain it to a tidy beginning and a happy ending. But the once-crystal-clear line between "then" and "now" blurs a little more every day.

The truth of it is, I am still living this story. And therein lies the hope.

ACKNOWLEDGEMENTS

Thank you Mama for making me write every single day of my homeschool career. It is because of you, I have a deep love for writing. I am eternally grateful.

Thank you Noah for always supporting me with my writing, for single parenting hundreds of hours while I ran off to do it, and for letting me tell the hard truth.

Thank you Renee for sitting with me in the early stages and championing my story onto paper.

Thank you Sheryl for taking my words, turning them inside out and into something better than I could have imagined.

Thank you Mandy for your big picture edits, Caroline for your thoughts and encouragement, and Brit for your keen eye.

Thank you to Julianna for your thoughtful suggestions but also for seeing me.

Thank you to Amy, Ashlee, Julia, Julie, and Rebekah for taking my heart on paper and devouring it. You gave me hope.

Thank you to Sam for making publishing this book a joyful experience.

Thank you Aunt Carolyn for finding Sam.

Thank you to every brave woman who shared her story with me. They were not shared in vain.

ABOUT THE AUTHOR

Helen Joy George resides in the beautiful mountains of Western North Carolina with her husband and three children. She spends her days writing, wading in the cool water of the rivers, and telling stories through photographs. She lives her life dealing with the ups and downs of bipolar disorder and is passionate about bringing awareness to the struggles of others with mental illness. This book is her heart.

www.helenjoy.com

Instagram: @helenjoygeorge

Email: authorhelenjoygeorge@gmail.com

CPSIA information can be obtained
at www.ICGtesting.com
Printed in the USA
BVHW072126151222
654334BV00007B/334